Accounting
and
Finance

Howell E. Jackson
James S. Reid, Jr., Professor of Law
Harvard Law School

Reprinted from
Analytical Methods for Lawyers

© 2004 By FOUNDATION PRESS

       395 Hudson Street

       New York, NY 10014

       Phone Toll Free 1–877–888–1330

       Fax (212) 367–6799

       fdpress.com

Printed in the United States of America

ISBN 1–58778–846–2

 TEXT IS PRINTED ON 10% POST CONSUMER RECYCLED PAPER

Preface

Lawyers in all areas of practice routinely confront issues of accounting and finance. Attorneys who draft employment agreements must understand the financial statements upon which compensation provisions and other contract terms often depend. Litigators presenting settlement offers to their clients must be able to explain financial aspects of the offers' terms and perhaps also speak to the credit-worthiness of the parties making the offers. Even family lawyers must have a basic understanding of financial issues in order to negotiate the fair division of assets in divorce proceedings or estate plans. To advise clients effectively in these and many other contexts, lawyers must possess at least a rudimentary understanding of the fields of accounting and finance. The goal of this handbook is to provide law students with these basic skills. The handbook is suitable for independent study and can also be used as a supplementary text for courses on corporate law, contracts, employment law, or other areas of study where students would benefit from a basic understanding of accounting or finance.

This handbook is drawn from Foundation Press's textbook, *Analytical Methods for Lawyers*, which was created to accompany a course several other professors and I have taught for the past five years at Harvard Law School. The course and the original text grew out of our joint realization that the traditional law school curriculum, with its focus on the development of analogical reasoning skills and legal writing and research, left many law students inadequately prepared for upper-level law courses and, more importantly, for legal practice in the modern world. Lawyers, whether corporate counsel or public interest advocates, must work in settings where effective argumentation and the giving of sound legal advice often depend on mastery of language and techniques derived from a range of disciplines that are staples of the modern business school curriculum but notably absent, in introductory form, from law school classrooms.

While some students arrive at law school well equipped with general knowledge of some of these areas from their undergraduate or work experience, many, perhaps the majority, of law students are woefully under-prepared in these areas. These students may self-select away from upper-level courses in which their inadequate preparation would disadvantage them. If so, they will graduate from law school without a set of basic skills, the absence of which will hamper their development in almost any of the careers that law graduates now pursue. Moreover, even those students who do have some general preparation in analytical methods are often unacquainted with how attorneys deploy these skills in practice. It has been our experience that many students are themselves acutely aware of their deficiencies in analytical methods (or are made aware of it when they encounter certain discussions in first-year classrooms or when they receive their first assignments in a summer job or internship). Such students are eager to have their legal education enhanced by material like that in this handbook, which promises to demystify analytical concepts and quantitative techniques that they see as clearly relevant to success in their law school coursework and, ultimately, to success in their chosen careers.

Unlike traditional introductory treatments, this handbook is not a dry or technical text, far removed from the world of law. Quite the opposite. Virtually every concept is introduced, explained, and applied in legal contexts. Additionally, this handbook is designed to be used to facilitate problem-based classroom discussion, materials for which are available to instructors in a Teachers' Manual. The translation from theory to practice is not left for students to develop on their own, after graduation. Instead, it is at the very heart of this handbook.

Cambridge, Massachusetts
September 2004

Contents

Accounting

1. Introduction

Contrary to what you may believe, there is nothing mysterious about accounting. It is simply a way of organizing financial information. Accounting offers a common language that can be used to communicate anything from a simple business plan of an entrepreneur seeking her first bank loan to the annual performance of an amateur theater company to a comprehensive rendering of the financial position of a multinational conglomerate. Lawyers of many sorts routinely deal with accounting statements. Family lawyers, litigators, government regulators, counsel to nonprofit organizations, labor lawyers, and even public-interest lawyers must work with financial statements as part of their day-to-day practices. Having a basic understanding of the language of financial accounting is thus a prerequisite to providing effective representation in all sorts of legal contexts.

Neither is there anything new about accounting. When Christopher Columbus first set sail across the Atlantic, one of his crew was a royal controller of accounts, assigned to the voyage to keep track of whatever gold and spice might be discovered. Our modern system of accounting can be traced back to the merchants of Florence and Venice in the fourteenth and fifteenth centuries. Prior methods of record keeping based on textual entries and Roman numerals were simply inadequate to deal with the explosion of trade and commercial activity that accompanied the European Renaissance. Modern accounting developed to fill this void.

Nor is accounting a monolithic discipline. Although many people associate accounting with the highly stylized (and often voluminous) financial statements that public corporations must distribute periodically to their shareholders, there are many other applications of accounting in our economy and legal system. Governmental entities have their own systems of financial statements, which are related to but distinct from the accounting conventions applied to entities in the private sector. Cost accounting is a subset of accounting rules designed to illuminate the costs of undertaking particular activities, whether developing a new form of medicine or mounting a fundraising effort for a local charity. A range of accounting conventions are routinely written into legal contracts, loan applications, applications for licenses and other government benefits, tax returns, and a host of other documents that lawyers are often called on to prepare. Although the specific accounting rules used vary from context to context, all are variants of a common language.

The first half of this chapter introduces the fundamentals of financial accounting. It begins with an overview of the three basic components of financial statements: the balance sheet, the income statement, and the summary of cash flows. The chapter then explores the double-entry bookkeeping system, upon which accounting statements are traditionally built, before turning to some of the conceptual foundations underlying modern accounting conventions. If you understand these basic principles, you will have a clear sense of both the strengths and the weaknesses of financial statements and an appreciation of the problems that recur in their creation and interpretation.

The second half of the chapter introduces more practical and institutional aspects of accounting. It discusses the legal and professional rules governing the creation of financial statements and then explores a more realistic example of financial statements. The chapter concludes by briefly introducing financial ratio analysis, a series of techniques that lawyers and financial analysts use to investigate and compare financial statements of different entities at different times.

2. Three Basic Accounting Formats

A typical financial statement has three components: a balance sheet, an income statement, and a summary of cash flows. Each provides a particular kind of information. To get a complete picture of an entity's overall financial status, lawyers routinely consult all three (as well as any related footnotes and textual descriptions accompanying financial statements). Before turning our sights to full-blown financial statements consisting of realistic examples of all three components, let's look at the basic concepts underlying the three formats by focusing on some simple examples.

A. Balance Sheets

In many respects, the most intuitive form of financial statement is the balance sheet. We can think of a balance sheet as a series of snapshots of an entity's financial position at specific times. A typical one includes two snapshots: one at the beginning of the period being reviewed (say, January 1) and one at the end of the period (say, December 31). By convention, information ordinarily is reported under three headings: assets, liabilities, and owners' equity. The asset side of the balance sheet of a hypothetical firm is presented in Figure 1 and the other side of the balance sheet — liabilities and owners' equity — in Figure 2.

1. Assets. The asset side of a firm's balance sheet is a listing of a firm's economic resources at a particular time. Under established accounting principles, assets are resources with "probable future economic benefits obtained or controlled by an entity resulting from past transactions or events." Although this definition may generally comport with the common understanding of the term *asset*, the accountant's definition has important peculiarities. To begin with, it has both retrospective and prospective elements. For an accountant to consider a resource an asset, (1) it must arise out of "past transactions or events," *and* (2) it must have "probable future economic benefits." In addition, it must be "owned or controlled" by the entity.

The accountant's definition of assets implicitly excludes a variety of resources that may be quite important to a firm's prospects. For example, resources with only a possibility — as opposed to probability — of yielding future benefits are not assets under the accountant's definition. In addition, resources must arise out of specific "past transactions or events" if they are to be considered assets. Thus, many important resources — e.g., inventions and other forms of intellectual property, reputation for providing good service, the CEO's sister-in-law being vice president of an important customer — do not meet the criteria for assets and typically would not be included on a firm's balance sheet.

Much can be learned from the asset side of even a simplified balance sheet, such as the one in Figure 1. For example, we can see that the firm's assets seem to have increased from $4.7 million at the beginning of the year to $5.6 million at the end. This sounds pretty good. But note that its cash has declined by $184,193 during the same period (the difference between its cash at the beginning of the year and its cash at the end of the year — i.e., $750,000 − $565,807 = $184,193). This may or may not be a good change, depending on how important it is for the firm to maintain substantial cash reserves and on what the firm did with the cash that is no longer on its balance sheet. If you were a lawyer whose client is expecting to be paid by this firm in the future, the decrease in cash reserves might raise concerns about the firm's ability to meet this obligation when it becomes due.

By convention, assets are listed in a particular order on balance sheets. Cash and things that are equivalent to cash (e.g., bank accounts) are listed first, and they are followed by other *current assets*. This category includes assets that are likely to be exchanged for cash in the relatively near future, typically within a year. For example, inventory available for sale is typically listed as a current asset, whereas an investment in real estate is usually not. More permanent assets (including plant, equipment, and other properties not likely to be sold soon) appear at the bottom of the asset side of the balance sheet.

A careful examination of a firm's balance sheet can reveal how each category of the firm's assets changed during the reporting period. Looking at Figure 1, can you figure out how much the firm's inventory changed during the year? (Hint: It increased.)

The lawyer's perspective

Suppose your client were the proprietor of a retail store having a substantial resource that was not represented on its balance sheets — for example, being located at the site where a new subway station was about to open. (Construction of a subway is not the sort of transaction or event that accountants would typically factor into financial statements.) In negotiating on your client's behalf for a bank loan, how could you persuade the bank that this resource was substantial? How could you assure the bank that it would not be dissipated before the loan was repaid? These questions have various possible answers. For example, you might present evidence about the market price of the property, or you might offer the store's commitment not to dispose of the property without the bank's permission. In neither case, however, would your client's balance sheet be particularly useful.

2. Liabilities and owners' equity. The other side of the firm's balance sheet — liabilities and owners' equity — is presented in Figure 2, again for both the beginning and the end of the period. This side of the balance sheet itemizes certain claims on the firm's resources, usually divided into claims of creditors (liabilities) and claims of the owners (owners' equity). Liabilities tend to be further divided into current liabilities (those likely to be reduced to cash payments within a year) and other liabilities (longer-term ones). For the typical U.S. corporation, where the owners are its shareholders, owners' equity consists of funds originally contributed by shareholders (capital stock in Figure 2) plus accumulated profits (retained earnings).

The terms *liabilities* and *owners' equity* have special meanings for accountants. Liabilities are defined as "probable future economic sacrifices of economic benefits arising from present

2836.18

Figure 1
Balance Sheet: Assets

	End of year	Start of year
Current assets		
Cash	$ 565,807	$ 750,000
Accounts receivable	1,000,000	825,000
Inventory	1,690,000	1,250,000
Prepaid expenses	160,000	185,000
Total current assets	**$3,415,807**	**$3,010,000**
Property, plant, and equipment		
Land, building, machines, equipment, and furniture	$3,000,000	$2,250,000
Accumulated depreciation	(800,000)	(540,000)
Cost less depreciation	**$2,200,000**	**$1,710,000**
Total assets	**$5,615,807**	**$4,720,000**

Adapted from Tracy, 1999, page 9.

obligations to transfer assets or render services in the future as a result of past transactions or events." A liability is thus the inverse of an asset. It arises out of an *obligation* incurred in the past, and it represents a *probable sacrifice* in the future. Accountants recognize many forms of liability, but not all future "sacrifices" of an entity will be encompassed by this definition. For example, a policy of retaining workers during recessions may result in a future sacrifice, yet the sacrifice may not arise out of a present obligation (e.g., if the employment relationship is an at-will one). Similarly, there may be a chance that a firm will be forced to pay a million dollar punitive damage award in a pending lawsuit; however, despite the substantial sacrifice that such a payment would represent, it would not be included as a liability on the balance sheet if the accountants conclude (in consultation with lawyers) that the award is not sufficiently likely to be made.

The accountant's definition of owners' equity derives from the two previous definitions: it is the "residual interest in assets of an entity after subtracting its liabilities." For this reason, the sum of total liabilities and owners' equity is always exactly equal to to-

Figure 2
Balance Sheet: Liability and Owners' Equity

	End of year	Start of year
Current liabilities		
Accounts payable	$ 640,000	$ 535,000
Accrued expenses	257,167	197,500
Income tax payable	23,940	36,000
Short-term notes payable	625,000	600,000
Total current liabilities	**$1,546,107**	**$1,368,500**
Long-term notes payable	$ 750,000	$ 600,000
Total liabilities	**$2,296,107**	**$1,968,500**
Stockholders' equity		
Capital stock (200,000 shares at end of year and 195,000 shares at start of year)	$ 775,000	$ 725,000
Retained earnings	2,544,700	2,026,500
Total owners' equity	**$3,319,700**	**$2,751,500**
Total liabilities and stockholders' equity	**$5,615,807**	**$4,720,000**

Adapted from Tracy, 1999, page 9.

tal assets. This relationship is referred to as the *fundamental equation of accounting.* Although this phenomenon may seem a miraculous coincidence to novices, it is simply a function of the way balance sheets are constructed: through a series of conventions known as double-entry bookkeeping (which we will take a closer look at later in the chapter). Does the fundamental equation hold true for the balance sheets in Figures 1 and 2?

B. Income Statements

The second component of a financial statement is the income statement. (A sample income statement for the hypothetical firm whose balance sheets we just considered appears in Figure 3.) Unlike balance sheets (which present snapshots of a firm's condition at particular times), the income statement provides a summary of financial activity over time, again typically a year (see Box 1). More specifically, it summarizes revenues and expenses during an accounting period. When revenues exceed expenses, as in the income statement in Figure 3, the entity is said to have earned a profit (e.g., $718,200 for the period documented in Figure 3). When expenses exceed revenues, the entity has suffered a loss. Hence, income statements are sometimes called *profit and loss statements*. In other contexts, they are referred to as *results of operations*.

The foregoing description of income statements is deceptively simple, because, in reality, these reports harbor much of the complexity of financial accounting. What are revenues and expenses? How are they allocated to particular periods? What is the relationship between a balance sheet and the corresponding income statement? Which is more important for assessing the financial health of an entity? Exactly which lines in the income statement should analysts focus on in assessing the health or potential of companies? Before we address these questions, let's focus on a few fairly straightforward features of income statements.

First, income statements typically begin with a measure of total revenue (e.g., sales revenue in Figure 3), from which is deducted a figure roughly equal to the direct cost of producing this revenue. For a manufacturing firm (such as the one whose income statement is in Figure 3), the direct cost is usually denominated *cost of goods sold*. Subtracting the direct cost from sales revenue

Figure 3
Income Statement

Sales revenue	$10,400,000
Cost of goods sold expense	(6,760,000)
Gross margin	$ 3,640,000
Operating expenses	$ (2,080,000)
Depreciation expenses	(260,000)
Operating earnings	$ 1,300,000
Interest expense	$ (103,000)
Earnings before income tax	$ 1,197,000
Income tax expense	$ (478,800)
Net income	$ 718,200

Adapted from Tracy, 1999, page 10.

Box 1
The Income Statement

The income statement is designed to reflect an entity's financial performance during some period of time. Its central feature is the comparison of the entity's revenues and expenses during the relevant period. Revenues and expenses are critical terms for accountants.

Revenues are defined as "increases in equity resulting from asset increases and/or liability decreases from delivering goods or services or other activities that constitute the entity's ongoing major or central operations."

Expenses are defined as "decreases in equity from asset decreases or liability increases from delivery of goods or services, or carrying out any activities which constitute the entity's ongoing major or central operations."

---

yields the *gross margin,* a measure of profitability. A firm, however, incurs a number of additional expenses in the course of doing business, and to determine the net income for the period, all of these must be deducted from the gross margin. By convention, accountants usually first subtract operating expenses (e.g., salary and administrative expenses) and depreciation (a charge for use of certain kinds of capital investments), to arrive at operating earnings and then deduct financial expenses (most importantly, interest charges on loans or other forms of borrowing) and income tax. After all these calculations are performed, the final remainder is the net income (or profit). If expenses exceed revenues during the period, net income will be negative and the entity will have suffered a loss. Depending on the nature of the entity and the preferences of the accountant preparing the statement, the designations of line items of an income statement can vary considerably. However, the basic structure of all income statements is the same: total revenues reduced by a cascade of expenses.

A second fundamental point about income statements has to do with their relationship to balance sheets. When a balance sheet is constructed, net income for the period is, in essence, added to retained (or accumulated) earnings. As a result, for a typical corporation net income ends up being included in owners' equity, which conforms with our intuition that a corporation's profits belong to its shareholders. Retained earnings can either be left in the corporation for future use or distributed to shareholders (as a dividend or in some other form). The hypothetical firm we have been discussing had a net income of $718,200, and it paid $200,000 in dividends to shareholders (this figure, which is not available from the statements we have looked at so far, appears in the summary of cash flows in Figure 4, which we will look at shortly). Hence, its retained earnings increased by $518,200 during the year ($718,200 − $200,000 = $518,200). We can confirm this fact by looking again at Figure 2 and noting that the firm's retained earnings did indeed increase by this amount ($2,544,700 − $2,026,500 = $518,200). (If this example is confusing, don't worry. Getting a firm grasp on the relationship between a balance sheet and the corresponding income statements takes time.)

The lawyer's perspective

Frequently, attorneys have to incorporate the concept of profit or loss into legal documents. If a client were the author of a best-selling novel and wanted to sell the movie rights for a percentage of the film's profits, the lawyer would have to translate this concept into a contractual term. Similarly, a plaintiff seeking to recover damages for a fire that prevented a factory from operating for a year would have to prove how much had been lost in profits as a result. Concepts of these sorts are also employed outside the commercial context. For example, if you represented a charitable institution that was thinking of hiring a new fundraising director, you might have to advise it about how to determine whether this person would make a net contribution (akin to profit) for the organization.

C. Summaries of Cash Flows

The third basic form of accounting format is the summary of cash flows. Like an income statement, a summary of cash flows reports financial performance during some period. Whereas an income statement summarizes a firm's profitability, a summary of cash flows highlights the manner in which the entity obtains and uses cash. Our hypothetical firm's summary of cash flows appears in Figure 4; it covers the same period as the income statement in Figure 3.

The purpose of the summary of cash flows is to illuminate the changes in an entity's cash position during an accounting period. When we were looking at balance sheets, we noted that the cash balance of our hypothetical firm had declined by $184,193 during the year in question. The final line in the summary of cash flows in Figure 4, which in its final line reports a $184,193 decrease in cash during the period, confirms this fact. Although this information can be gleaned from both documents, the summary of cash flows provides much more detail about the factors that contributed to the change. The statement begins with the firm's net income for the period, $718,200 (as reported in the income statement in Figure 3). Net income is adjusted to account for changes during the reporting period in balance sheet entries related to operations. Such adjustments are in reality a bit complex. In general, however, increases in assets (and decreases in liabilities) use up cash and therefore are entered as negative numbers (i.e., they are cash outflows). For example, when a company buys additional inventory or pays off a loan, it uses up cash reserves. On the other hand, decreases in assets (and increases in liabilities) are positive numbers, because they add to the entity's cash. For example, when a firm sells inventory or takes out a loan, it increases its cash reserves. On balance, these adjustments in our

Figure 4
Summary of Cash Flows

Cash flows from operating expenses

Net income		$ 718,200
Accounts receivable increase	$(175,000)	
Inventory increase	(440,000)	
Prepaid expenses decrease	25,000	
Depreciation expense	260,000	
Accounts payable increase	105,000	
Accrued expenses increase	59,667	
Income tax payable decrease	(12,060)	
Cash flow adjustments to net income		$(177,393)
Cash flow from operating activities		$ 540,807

Cash flows from investing activities

Purchase of property, plant, and equipment		$(750,000)

Cash flows from financial activities

Short-term debt borrowing	$ 25,000	
Long-term debt borrowing	150,000	
Capital stock issue	50,000	
Dividends paid stockholders	(200,000)	
Cash flow adjustments for financial activities		$ 25,000
Increase (Decrease) in cash during year		**$(184,193)**

Adapted from Tracy, 1999, page 18.

hypothetical firm's operating accounts used up $177,393 in cash and thereby reduced its cash flow from operations to $540,807 ($718,200 − $177,393 = $540,807).

By convention, summaries of cash flows also include information on cash used for longer-term investments (as opposed to operating activities) as well as information on cash flows associated with financial activities, such as borrowing money or paying dividends. The summary in Figure 4 indicates that during the year our hypothetical firm used $750,000 in cash to invest in the physical plant, that is, had a cash outflow of $750,000 for this purpose. The summary also shows a net inflow of $25,000 from financial operations. Although the company actually took in $225,000 in cash (through new borrowings and by issuing capital stock), this figure was offset by an outflow of $200,000 in cash as dividends paid to stockholders. (These were the dividends mentioned earlier.)

Taken together, the summaries of cash flows in this financial statement offer a fairly complete answer to the question posed earlier about changes in the firm's cash position during the year. Its cash reserves may have decreased, but the decrease does not seem to be cause for concern. The firm was profitable (it made $718,200 last year), and even after adjusting for changes in associated accounts, its operations generated a decent amount of cash ($540,807). The principal reason for the decline in its cash reserves was its investment of $750,000 in new plant and equipment. Unless such an investment were to be made again during the following reporting period — we would have to investigate further to know for sure whether or not it would be — we would expect cash reserves to rebound next year. Moreover, the expenditure of $750,000 in new plant and equipment might even enhance the company's ability to generate additional income in the future.

As might be obvious from the foregoing, a summary of cash flows is largely derived from information in an entity's balance sheets and income statement, and for now we will focus on these two other accounting formats. Summaries of cash flows are, nevertheless, extremely useful tools when an entity's liquidity (its ability to make payments on time) is the topic of interest. In many legal contexts, such as when an entity is financially strapped, its liquidity is paramount. And, as will become obvious in the Finance chapter, financial analysts are particularly interested in firms' cash flows.

3. Double-Entry Bookkeeping
and the Accountant's Frame of Reference

The three basic categories of financial statement — balance sheets, income statements, and summaries of cash flows — are the ones with which lawyers typically deal. Although lawyers are not usually responsible for creating these statements — doing so is the province of accountants — lawyers should have a basic understanding of how accountants go about doing the job so that they can appreciate the nature of financial statements and have some insight into what information can and cannot be found in them.

A. The Transactional Nature of Financial Statements

As you may remember, the accountant's definitions of assets and liabilities spoke in terms of resources and obligations arising out of past transactions or events. The attention to specific transactions and events stems from an important aspect of the logic that underlies accounting. Financial statements reflect an accumulation of transactions and events, which accountants record in accordance with certain conventions that have evolved over time. Typically, the transactions and events are initially recorded as temporary entries in *journals* or *T accounts*. Then, at the end of the accounting period, these accounts are *closed*, and the balances are transferred to the appropriate places on the entity's financial statements.

We will consider in a moment the manner in which these accounting entries are made. But as a preliminary matter, a bias inherent in the transactional foundation of accounting bears noting. It is best explained by example: When a company buys a piece of equipment or sells a widget, a transaction has occurred, and it will be recorded in T accounts and eventually reflected in the firm's financial statements. On the other hand, when consumer tastes change or the price of raw materials rises, such an event, even if of critical importance to the entity's financial health, typically does not constitute a transaction or event that is registered as an entry in the T accounts and therefore is not likely to be reflected in the firm's financial statements. This is one reason why financial statements may not present a complete picture of a firm's economic condition. (Although the reference here is to T accounts, other discussions of bookkeeping procedures may speak in terms of journal entries, which perform essentially the same function as T accounts.)

Box 2
Debits and Credits

For many students learning accounting for the first time, the way accountants use the terms debit and credit is counterintuitive and confusing. One reason for this confusion is that students often associate *credit* with positive and *debit* with negative.

Accountants have almost the opposite frame of reference. For example, on the liabilities side of the balance sheet, a credit entry increases a firm's liabilities. The logic is that an increase in liabilities is an increase in the amount the firm owes its creditors. Similarly an increase in assets is a debit entry on the grounds that the greater the amount the firm's debtors owe, the greater the firm's assets.

In terms of understanding how financial accounts are created, it's probably best to dispense with any preconceived notions about the meaning of debit and credit. Remembering their physical location in journal entries is much more helpful: debit entries are always on the left-hand side of T accounts and credit entries are always on the right-hand side. It is this fact that ensures that the fundamental accounting equation always remains true.

B. The Logic of Double-Entry Bookkeeping

Double-entry bookkeeping is the system that accountants use to record transactions and events. As the phrase suggests, each transaction or event is recorded twice, once as a debit entry and once as a credit entry (see Box 2). It is because of this *double-entry* convention that the fundamental accounting equation always holds. The easiest way to see how this relationship works is to think of how transactions affect a balance sheet. Suppose a company received a $100 loan from its bank. The accountant would record this transaction as a $100 increase in the company's cash (i.e., an increase in assets) and an offsetting $100 increase in the firm's borrowings (an increase in liabilities).

Every time an asset is added (which would constitute a debit entry), either another asset must be reduced or a liability account or owners' equity must be increased (either action would be a credit entry). Conversely, increasing a liability account or owners' equity (making a credit entry) requires either that another liability account or owners' equity account be decreased or that an asset account be increased (either of which would be a debit entry). This description may seem obscure on first reading, but it should become clearer as we work through some examples.

Example 1

Suppose that a company used $100 of cash to purchase inventory. The bookkeeping entries would consist of a credit

Example 1: T Accounts

Cash	
dr	cr
	$100 purchase of inventory

Inventory	
dr	cr
$100 purchase of inventory	

(decrease) to cash of $100 and a debit (increase) of the same amount to inventory.

Example 2

Suppose that the firm then borrowed $200 from a bank to acquire a piece of land. The bookkeeping entries for this transaction would be a credit (increase) to a liability account to represent the loan and a debit (increase) to an asset account to represent the property.

Example 2: T Accounts

Land		Loan	
dr	cr	dr	cr
$200 purchase of land with loan			$200 loan for land

Example 3

Suppose that the firm used $50 of cash to repay a portion of the loan. The bookkeeping entries would show a $50 credit to (reduction in) the firm's cash and a $50 debit to (decrease in) the loan account, as indicated by the italicized boldfaced entries.

Example 3: T Accounts

Cash		Loan	
dr	cr	dr	cr
	$100 purchase of inventory	*$50 repayment of loan*	$200 loan for land
	$50 repayment of loan		

Another peculiarity of double-entry bookkeeping is that transactional entries can be made either to balance sheet accounts or to accounts related to the income statement. (If you look at Box 1 again, you will see that revenues and expenses are defined in terms of transactions that affect both the equity account and the asset or liability accounts.) Entries for transactions involving revenue or expenses are posted to the income statement when the accounts are closed at the end of the reporting period.

Example 4

Suppose that the firm from the previous examples sold all of its inventory for $200 in cash. Accountants would record this as two separate transactions: (1) as a $200 increase in cash (debit) plus an offsetting $200 increase in revenue (credit), and (2) as a $100 reduction in (credit to) inventory plus a $100 increase in (debit to) cost of goods sold. These are the entries that are in italicized boldface type below.

Example 4: T Accounts

Cash		Sales revenue	
dr	cr	dr	cr
$200 receipt from sale (1)	$100 purchase of inventory		*$200 receipt from sale (1)*
	$50 repayment of loan		

Inventory		Cost of goods sold	
dr	cr	dr	cr
$100 purchase of inventory	*$100 disposition of inventory (2)*	*$100 disposition of inventory (2)*	

You may be puzzled about how the fundamental accounting equation can hold in Example 4, given that half of some entries are allocated to accounts of the income statement rather than the total being applied to balance sheet accounts. There are various ways of explaining this. One way is as follows: At the end of the accounting period, when the T accounts are closed and the appropriate items are posted to the income statement, a final profit or loss is calculated. This figure represents the difference between revenues and expenses allocated to T accounts associated with the income statement accounts during the reporting period. The profit or loss figure is then transferred to the retained earnings account on the balance sheet, creating a debit or credit sufficient to restore balance to the financial statement. (An in-class exercise should illuminate this point).

C. Closing Out T Accounts

As suggested earlier, T accounts are only provisional entries. At the end of each accounting period, these accounts are closed out, and the net balances are transferred to the firm's financial statements. To see how this works, look again at the examples given above. As summarized in Example 4, three separate transactions affected the T account for cash: (1) $100 was deducted (credited) to represent the purchase of inventory; (2) $50 was deducted (credited) to account for the loan repayment; and (3) $200 was added (debited) to reflect the receipt of sales revenue. If an accountant were to close this account, it would show a net increase (debit) of $50. As a result, during the accounting period, the firm's cash increased by $50. And, if a new balance sheet were generated, the firm's cash account would be $50 greater than it was at the beginning of the period.

The accountant would close out every other T account in a similar way. Some account balances would be transferred to the asset side of the firm's balance sheet; others would be posted to the liability side or to owners' equity. One tricky aspect to this process is knowing which accounts are posted first to the firm's income statement, where they are factored into the calculation of net income or loss and then transferred back to a balance sheet account such as retained earnings. The key to figuring out which accounts are treated in this special manner are the definitions of revenues and expenses given in Box 1.

The lawyer's perspective

Although lawyers are seldom responsible for maintaining double-entry bookkeeping accounts, they often play a role in ensuring that a client's internal accounting procedures are adequate to detect and prevent fraudulent activity. An unscrupulous sales manager could easily disguise poor performance by classifying too many transactions as entries for revenue accounts or too few as entries for expense accounts. Accordingly, a fundamental principle of internal control is to keep operational responsibilities separate from accounting responsibilities. To protect a client's interests, lawyers often are responsible for ensuring that such separation is maintained.

4. Some Fundamental Concepts

Now let's pull back a bit from the details we've been looking at and focus instead on the major principles and assumptions that underlie financial accounting — the critical lessons of this chapter. This information can be organized into four categories: the big picture, the conservative bias of financial statements, the matching principle and its implications, and boundary problems.

A. The Big Picture

Let's begin with a few points that may strike you as obvious but that are sufficiently important to warrant explicit notation.

1. The entity concept. An initial point to be made about financial statements is that they concern a particular entity — a corporation and not its shareholders, a partnership and not its suppliers or customers, and so on. Although this may seem intuitive when the entity is a large public corporation such as IBM, which has tens of thousands of shareholders, the division between owners and corporations can be less well defined for smaller entities or start-up ventures. For example, when a couple of young entrepreneurs establish a firm and operate the business in their garage, is the garage an asset of the firm or of its shareholders? What if the garage is leased by the firm for a dollar a year? For a million dollars a year?

The accounting profession has a number of conventions for reporting transactions between firms and related parties (such as owners and principal employees). This is also an area of particular scrutiny in federal securities regulation, corporate law, and the income taxation system, as the transactions between related parties present fertile ground for manipulation and abuse. Beyond these applications, however, the entity concept is an important building block for lawyers because it reveals a basic truth about legal obligations and the likelihood that they will be honored. In interactions with a legal entity, the resources of only that entity are presumptively available to stand behind its obligations. For example, a contract with a subsidiary of a large multinational corporation does not necessarily — or even ordinarily — represent a legal commitment on the part of the parent corporation or any other affiliate. For this reason, it is important for attorneys to focus on the financial wherewithal of the specific legal entity that enters into a contract. Financial statements are well suited to help them do so.

The lawyer's perspective

Suppose that your client were about to enter into a food-service contract with the subsidiary of a large firm and was concerned about the subsidiary's relatively modest balance sheet. How could you improve the likelihood that your client would be paid for the services it was about to provide?

2. The fundamental accounting equation. Although the basic accounting equation has already been stated (and subsequently referred to more than once), it is important enough to warrant repetition: *owners' equity is the amount by which a firm's total assets exceeds its total liabilities.* Or, with modest algebraic reformulation, *total assets* are, by definition, equal to the sum of a firm's total liabilities and owners' equity. These equations are true not just of corporations but also of nonprofit organizations, such as schools and religious organizations. The only difference is that outside the corporate realm owners' equity is associated, not usually with shareholders, but with other groups of claimants or residual owners. For this reason, in the context of nonprofits, the analogous accounting entry may be labeled *accumulated surplus* or *net assets*. Whatever label is used, the entry constitutes the difference between the entity's total assets and its total liabilities.

Figure 5 is a common graphical presentation of the fundamental accounting equation. For a variety of reasons, lawyers find it useful to keep this image in mind. For example, if a client is about to enter into a business contract with a firm, it is important for the attorney to know how many other obligations the firm has already undertaken — that is, what other liabilities are outstanding. In addition, it is wise for the attorney to have a sense of the comparative magnitudes of those liabilities and the firm's assets. For a firm with $10 million of assets, liabilities of $1 million would not be troubling, whereas for a firm whose balance sheet shows $500,000 in assets, $10 million in liabilities should raise some eyebrows. (What would the owners' equity be? Hint: Owners' equity can be negative.)

Occasionally, lawyers speak in terms of trying to move a client's interests up the right-hand side of a firm's balance sheet. They simply mean that they are attempting to improve the status of the client's claim relative to that of other claims against the firm. (On a balance sheet, more senior liabilities are typically listed above junior claims, and short-term debts — liabilities to be repaid within a year — are at the top.) The seniority (i.e., priority) of a creditor can be altered by contract if the other creditors agree to subordinate their claims — that is, if the other creditors authorize the company to pay off that creditor first. Alternatively, a corporation or individual borrower can pledge specific assets as collateral for certain claims. Under such an arrangement, the "secured" creditor has a special claim on those assets, which can be used to ensure that its obligation is repaid. Our bankruptcy system offers a statutory mechanism for sorting out the relative order of claims of creditors when an entity can neither honor all of its

Figure 5
The Fundamental Accounting Equation

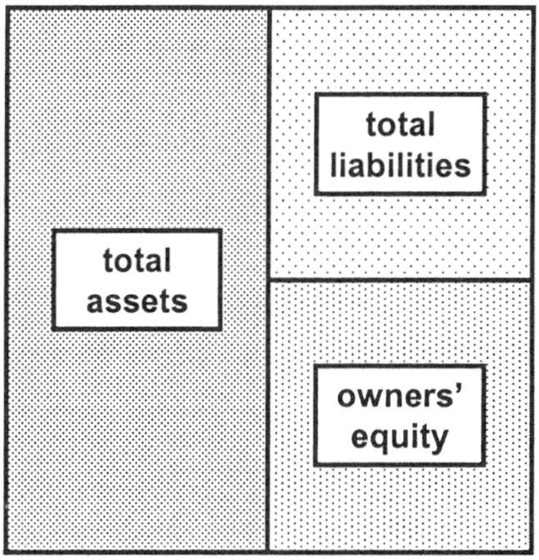

owners' equity = total assets − total liabilities
total assets = total liabilities + owners' equity

obligations as they become due nor work out an alternative mechanism for repayment to which all creditors are willing to agree. (Upper-level law school courses on commercial law and bankruptcy dedicate considerable time to these topics.)

B. The Conservative Bias of Accountants

During their training, accountants are encouraged to take a conservative, even skeptical posture with respect to the creation of financial statements. In part, this perspective reflects the profession's role as a counterweight to the tendency of individuals and firms to gravitate toward presenting their financial condition in the best possible light. But the conservative bias of accountants does affect the kinds of information they include in financial statements, and it is a factor that lawyers must appreciate and keep in mind when using financial statements. We have already seen one illustration of this phenomenon — the accountant's definitions of assets and liabilities, which restrict financial statements to resources and obligations arising out of past transactions or events. Here are two others:

1. The monetary unit concept. You may have noticed that all of the accounting entries we have discussed so far have been denominated in dollars. This is no coincidence. Under a convention known as the monetary unit concept, accountants are required to express all figures in a common monetary unit. So you will never see balance sheet entries expressed in terms of nonmonetary units (e.g., 10 bales of hay or 5 acres of land). Because of this accounting convention, accountants are reluctant to record occurrences that are not easily convertible to monetary units, such as changes in consumer taste.

2. Preference for historical costs over market values. Another traditional feature of financial accounting is a preference to rely on historical (i.e., original) cost rather than market value. For example, if a company purchased a piece of land in 1950 for $100,000, that land could still be recorded on the firm's financial statements half a century later as having the same value, even if its current market value exceeded $1 million or even $10 million.

The preference for using historic cost rather than market value may strike you as odd, but it provides some insight into the logic that underlies accounting. In an environment of gradually (or even rapidly) rising prices, historical cost tends to be more conservative, at least in assigning value to assets such as land. Moreover, historic costs tend to be based on actual transactions (e.g., in the preceding example, the $100,000 paid for the land in 1950). In many contexts, reliance on market value is more subjective and susceptible to manipulation. For example, the valuation of works of fine art is highly subjective; claiming that an art collection has great value doesn't make it so. Furthermore, having to repeatedly recalculate market price could substantially complicate the accountant's task.

The divergence between historical cost and market value introduces another disconnect, in today's vernacular, between financial statements and economic reality. When the historical cost significantly deviates from the current market value of an asset, the balance sheet does not offer an accurate reflection of the firm's financial health, and even the income statement can become misleading in certain respects. For this reason, some academic writers have argued that accounting principles should be reformulated to reflect market value (or sometimes replacement cost) instead of historical cost. And, in some areas, such as the valuation of certain financial assets with readily defined market values, accountants are sometimes required to use market value in preparing financial statements. The norm in most areas of accounting, however, remains historical cost.

C. The Matching Principle and Its (Profound) Implications

Another important tenet of accounting is the matching principle, according to which

- revenue should be allocated to the period during which effort is expended in generating it, and
- an expense should be allocated to the period in which the benefit from it will contribute to income generation

This principle and related concepts determine when transactions should be recorded as entries in revenue or expense accounts. (You might want to look back at the earlier discussion of double-entry bookkeeping). The matching principle accords with the intuition that an income statement is intended to summarize economic activity within a particular period. To do so, it must reflect all revenues and associated expenses from that period but no others.

If all transactions were completed within a single time period and if all items of input were consumed within a single period, the matching principle would be fairly easy to implement. Reality, however, is more complex. Customers buy products in one period and pay for them in the next. Companies purchase equipment that lasts for many years and contributes to revenue generation in multiple accounting periods. To deal with this messiness, accountants rely on yet additional conventions: *accrual* and *deferral*. These conventions allow accountants to allocate revenues and expenses to the appropriate time period even though cash payments for the associated transactions may not be received until a subsequent period and even though cash expenditures for some relevant inputs may have been made in earlier periods.

We will explore a few important examples of these concepts shortly. For the moment, what you should appreciate as a future lawyer who will have to make use of financial statements is that inherently discretionary judgment calls are an unavoidable outgrowth of the matching principle. Although accountants have many detailed rules governing accrual and deferral — and much professional effort has gone into making these rules as formally realizable as possible — the ultimate decision as to when revenues should be recognized or expenses allocated remains a matter of judgment. If a client's interests depend on a calculation of profit or loss, the attorney has to consider who is allocating the revenues and expenses from the underlying transactions and how that person's decisions will be monitored.

1. Recognition of income. By now, it is probably clear that income can be recognized (i.e., recorded in revenue accounts of an income statement) in various ways. Let's look at some examples by way of illustration.

Example 5

Assume that we are dealing with a law firm that has three clients: A, B, and C. The firm does work for Client A in Year 1, who stops by the firm before the year is over to settle the account by paying $100 in cash. The firm also does work for Client B in Year 1, but sends Client B a bill for $200, which Client B has not paid by the end of the year. The firm does no work for Client C in Year 1 but does receive a retainer of $300 from this client, with the understanding that Client C will use the firm's services in Year 2. Under the matching principle, how should the firm account for each of these transactions?

Client A. This example is fairly straightforward, as all relevant activity occurs in Year 1. Accordingly, the appropriate treatment is to recognize revenue of $100 in that period. Under double-entry bookkeeping, the cash account would be debited (increased by) $100 and the revenue account credited for (also increased by) the same amount.

Example 5a: T Account Entries for Client A

Cash		Revenues	
dr	cr	dr	cr
$100 payment for services		$100 payment for services	

Client B. In terms of the firm's effort, the work for Client B occurred during the same period as the work for Client A; as of year end, however, Client B's payment had not been made. In order to honor the matching principle, the firm's accountant has to have some way to recognize the revenue in Year 1, even though the bill remains outstanding. The standard way of handling this problem is by using an asset account known as accounts receivable (bills outstanding on which payment is expected shortly). So, to record the transactions with Client B, the law firm's revenue account would be credited for (increased by) $200, and the offsetting entry would be a $200 debit to (increase in) accounts receivable. Then, when the bill is paid, presumably in Year 2, cash will be debited (increased) and accounts receivable credited (decreased), with no effect on the firm's income statement for Year 2.

Example 5b: T Account Entries for Client B

Accounts receivable		Revenues	
dr	cr	dr	cr
$200 billing of services		$200 billing of services	

Client C. This situation is the obverse of the preceding example. The firm receives cash but renders no services in Year 1. To adhere to the matching principle in this case, the accountant has to be able to note the receipt of cash in Year 1 but postpone the recognition of income to Year 2. A technique known as deferral is available for doing just this. The accountant would turn to a liability account known as deferred income. (It is a liability because it represents an obligation to be met in the future.) The bookkeeping entries would be as follows: the receipt of the money in Year 1 would constitute a debit to (increase in) cash of $300 and a credit for (increase of) the same amount to deferred income. In Year 2, when the firm provides the promised services, deferred income will be debited (reduced by) $300 and the revenue account credited for (increased by) $300. Hence, the transaction would be factored into the firm's income statement for Year 2.

Example 5c: T Account Entries for Client C

Cash		Deferred Income	
dr	cr	dr	cr
$300 retainer			$300 retainer

2. Allocation of expenditures under accrual accounting. Similar complexities arise in the allocation of expenditures to expense accounts. As with the income recognition problems outlined above, the root of these difficulties is that cash payments for inputs necessary to generate income are not always made in the period during which the associated revenue is generated. The rules of accounting in this area are extraordinarily complex, and we will limit our discussion to two prominent illustrations.

a. Cost of goods sold. Our first example concerns the rules that govern the valuation of inventory purchased over time at various prices. Suppose that a firm enters into the business of supplying home heating oil and builds a new storage tank capable of holding 1,000 gallons. In Year One, it fills the tank with oil purchased at $1.00 a gallon (1) and sells half of its inventory during the year (2). At the beginning of Year Two, the firm replenishes its inventory by purchasing 500 gallons at $2.00 a gallon (3) and during the year sells 500 gallons (4).

The accounting treatment for Year One is fairly straightforward (see Figure 6). The company's initial purchase of 1,000 gallons of oil constitutes a $1,000 decrease (credit) of cash offset by a $1,000 increase (debit) in inventory. Then the sale of 500 gallons reduces (credits) inventory by $500, with an offsetting increase (debit) to cost of goods sold, which is an expense account.

The first transaction in Year Two is also uncomplicated. The further purchase of 500 gallons of heating oil at $2 a gallon reduces (credits) cash by $1,000 and increases (debits) inventory by the same amount. But how should the accountant deal with the sale of 500 gallons in Year Two? The accountant could use the

Figure 6
Inventory with Two Alternatives: T Accounts

Cash		Cost of goods sold	
dr	cr	dr	cr
	$1,000 purchase of 1,000 gallons of oil at $1/gallon (1)	$500 sale of oil at $1/gallon (2)	
	$1,000 purchase of 500 gallons of oil at $2/gallon (3)	$500 sale of oil at $1/gallon (4a)	
		$1,000 sale of oil at $2/gallon (4b)	

Inventory	
dr	cr
$1,000 purchase of oil at $1/gallon (1)	$500 sale of oil at $1/gallon (2)
$1,000 purchase of oil at $2/gallon (3)	$500 sale of 500 gallons of oil at $1/gallon (4a)
	$1,000 sale of 500 gallons of oil at $2/gallon (4b)

earlier price of oil first — the so-called FIFO (first-in, first-out) approach — that is, value the oil sold in Year Two at $1.00 a gallon (4a). Alternatively, the accountant could use the most recent price of inventory — known as LIFO (last-in, first out) — and assign a value of $2.00 per gallon (4b). What are the advantages and disadvantages of each of these methods? Can you think of other ways to approach this problem? Which would be most consistent with the underlying logic of financial accounting?

b. *Capitalization and depreciation of expenditures.* A related issue arises when inputs have readily determined costs (say, a computer purchased for $2,000) that contribute to income over several accounting periods. The problem here is figuring out, not what the appropriate cost of the input is, but when it should be reflected as an expense on the firm's income statement. Accountants solve this problem by allowing the capitalization of certain expenditures — that is, making them into assets — and then requiring them to be depreciated — reflected as expenses — over some fixed period that is supposed to correspond to the period during which the asset contributes to income generation.

In terms of bookkeeping, accountants do this by crediting (reducing) cash and debiting (increasing) equipment when the computer is purchased — neither of which transactions affects the firm's income statement. Then, over some predetermined period — say, five years — they make annual credits (deductions) to the equipment account and offsetting debits (increases) in an expense account for depreciation. So, for the preceding example, the computer would, as indicated in Figure 7, initially be capitalized as a $2,000 asset (1) and then be depreciated over five years, thereby generating an annual expense of $400 (one-fifth of $2,000) for each year (2). This combination of capitalization and depreciation allows accountants to match (more or less) the cost of purchased equipment to the periods during which the investment (i.e., the equipment) contributed to income.

Figure 7
Capitalization and Depreciation: T Accounts

```
                 Cash
_____
              dr | cr
                 | $2,000 purchase
                 | of equipment (1)
```

```
    Property, plant, and equipment                 Depreciation expense
_____    _____
              dr | cr                                      dr | cr
$2,000 purchase  | $400 depreciation         $400 depreciation  |
of equipment (1) | of equipment in            of equipment in   |
                 | Year One (2)                 Year One (2)     |
```

The lawyer's perspective

Lawyers do, in fact, spend a good deal of time advising clients on capitalization and depreciation. In certain contexts (such as when financial statements are prepared for the investment community), clients have a strong desire to capitalize expenditures in order to reduce or postpone expenses and thereby increase reported earnings. In other settings (e.g., when income is calculated for tax purposes) they are likely to be less inclined to capitalize expenditures or at least to be interested in the quickest possible system of depreciation. Why? Because they want to lower their reported income and thereby their income taxes. Lawyers often play a role in helping clients make these accounting decisions and may even be called on to structure contracts so that subsequent accounting treatments will be more advantageous to the clients' interests. How might this be done?

D. Boundary Problems

So far, we have focused on fairly concrete examples of assets and liabilities, such as computer equipment and bank loans. The classification of economic activity is not always so straightforward, and many cases fall within the gray area between items that are supposed to be included within financial statements and those that are not. Intangible assets, contingent liabilities, and "extraordinary and unusual items" are three such categories that lawyers have to be aware of.

1. Intangible assets. Early on, we noted that not all economic resources are treated as assets when it comes to balance sheets. Various sorts of intangible assets (i.e., ones that lack any physical substance) fall into this category. They include intellectual property (e.g., trademarks and patents), favorable reputations, a well-trained workforce, and other factors that contribute to a successful enterprise. Given the accountant's convention of using historical cost (as opposed to market valuation) and a preference for conservatism in the face of uncertainty, intangible assets typically appear on the balance sheet only to the extent that they are the products of identifiable costs. Thus, many intangible assets have no impact on a firm's financial statements, their considerable economic importance notwithstanding.

Intangible assets are treated differently, however, if they have been purchased by an entity in an arm's-length transaction. For example, the Coca-Cola trademark — an extremely valuable brand name — may not be recorded as a material asset on the firm's balance sheet. If, however, General Mills were to purchase the trademark from Coca-Cola for $10 billion in cash, it would be recorded on the General Mills balance sheet as having a value of $10 billion (and then might be slowly amortized as an expense on the firm's income statement the number of years deemed to reflect its useful life). Thus, the same piece of intellectual property would have no impact on one balance sheet and a $10 billion impact on another.

The lawyer's perspective

Suppose that you were general counsel for a firm that was interested in obtaining the services of Joey Winkle, a 13-year-old computer genius who had a reputation for designing web pages that attract millions of viewers. A year ago, Joey set up his own company, in which he was the only employee. To date, he has paid himself an annual salary of $10,000 and has used the rest of his company's revenues to purchase fast food and the latest computer games, most of which are already obsolete. You are considering two ways of structuring the deal: (1) entering into a five-year exclusive service contract with Joey's company for $100,000 a year or (2) purchasing the company outright for $450,000, with the understanding that Joey would continue working for the company until he begins college in five years. What are the accounting implications of each of these two choices?

2. Contingent liabilities. An analogous, but more profound problem confronts accountants when they face obligations that a firm might, but will not necessarily, incur — liabilities that are contingent on future events. As it turns out, a great deal of economic (and legal) activity falls into this category. Common examples include the financial guarantee (i.e., a promise to repay another person's debts), which comes due only if the other party defaults; the warranty, which requires performance only if a product malfunctions; or liability in a lawsuit, which arises only if the plaintiff prevails. In none of these examples is future payment a sure thing, but it is a possibility in all of them. The accountant must resolve the issue of how to reflect such situations on financial statements.

The solution that the accounting profession has developed to deal with contingent liabilities is multifaceted. When it is probable that the liability will be incurred and the cost can be reasonably estimated — that is, for the least contingent of contingent liabilities — firms are supposed to accrue the loss for financial reporting purposes. (Bookkeeping entries: credit [increase] a liability account on the balance sheet, and debit [increase] an expense item to be reflected in the firm's income statement for the reporting period.) When the contingency is reasonably possible (i.e., more than remote but less than probable) or when the loss is probable but no reasonable cost estimate can be made, the normal practice is to disclose information about the contingency (frequently also providing an estimated cost or range of costs) in a footnote on the financial statements and often elsewhere as well, such as in SEC disclosure documents.

The lawyer's perspective

One of the most frequent points of interaction between attorneys and accountants is the discussion of contingent liabilities and how they should be reported on financial statements. To help accountants classify pending legal claims, attorneys are often asked to assess the likely outcome of pending litigation as well as to estimate possible damage awards. In addition, accountants routinely send law firms letters listing all pending or threatened litigation that the accountants are aware of and requesting the firms to confirm that they are not aware of any other pending or threatened actions. Suppose that you received such a letter and it did not mention an environmental problem that you are currently working on, a problem for which the company has potentially substantial, but not yet fully ascertained, legal exposure. How should you respond to the accountant's letter?

3. **Extraordinary and unusual items.** Another interesting boundary problem concerns the treatment of costs associated with events that are highly unusual, such as natural disasters, exceptional legal awards, unexpected deterioration of business assets, and corporate transactions such as mergers and acquisitions. These costs are similar to expenses that would ordinarily be charged to an entity's income statement, but because they are unusual, they are not tied to firms' ordinary operations and are therefore not likely to recur. Accounting conventions call for such unusual and nonrecurrent items to be distinguished from other expenses on income statements. Typically, these items appear on a separate line, beneath a line denominated "net income before extraordinary and unusual items" or words to that effect.

In recent years, several prominent officials (including former SEC Chair Arthur Levitt) have criticized firms for treating too many costs as extraordinary and unusual items. Inasmuch as these charges reduce net income (and therefore owners' equity) for the period in which they are taken, why do you think firms might have an incentive to be overly aggressive in this area?

5. The Institutional and Legal Structure of Accounting

An important part of a lawyer's education about financial accounting is learning about the institutional and legal context in which accounting standards are developed and applied. So far in this chapter, we have discussed various principles underlying financial statements and the conventions for implementing them. But how are they agreed on, and to what extent are they legally binding on private parties? Lawyers have to understand these institutional arrangements as well as the accounting conventions they support.

A. Institutions and the Creation of Accounting Standards

In the United States, the government's role in the development of accounting standards is relatively limited. The SEC, a federal entity, does play a role in defining a wide range of information that public companies must supply to their shareholders (e.g., annual reports and on certain occasions other disclosure documents, such as those required when securities are sold to the general public). However, these rules apply to only a very small fraction of U.S. firms (only some 15,000 to 20,000 companies — less than 1% of all U.S. businesses) — at any given time. For these firms, the SEC has an elaborate system of disclosure requirements and accounting standards (known respectively as Regulation S-K and Regulation S-X). In addition, the SEC requires that the financial statements of public companies be maintained in accordance with a body of authority known as generally accepted accounting principles (GAAP, pronounced like the name of the store) and that these statements be reviewed (or audited) periodically by independent accounting firms.

In part because of the SEC's influence, GAAP has become the dominant accounting norm in this country. It either controls or heavily influences the accounting practices of nearly all firms that maintain financial statements in the U.S. — whether or not publicly owned — as well as an increasing number of entities in other jurisdictions. The conventions introduced during our discussion of accounting standards are, in fact, the basic elements of GAAP.

The institution primarily responsible for articulating GAAP is the Financial Accounting Standard Board (FASB, rhymes with frisbee). FASB, an independent organization founded in 1973 and located in Connecticut, comprises seven full-time board members, including prominent certified public accountants, corporate executives, financial analysts, and academics. Its articulates GAAP principally by issuing statements and interpretations. (For example, FASB Statement No. 5 deals with accounting for contingencies, whereas Interpretation No. 14 addresses reasonable estimation of losses.) Before FASB issues a new statement on a subject, the board typically appoints a task force to investigate the matter and engages in a prolonged period of notice-and-comment, during which interested parties (often including the SEC) provide input and reaction. FASB's statements and interpretative releases are the highest form of authority in the accounting profession, but they are supplemented by a host of lesser forms of guidance, including other sorts of FASB pronouncements as well as standards articulated by FASB's predecessor organization, the Accounting Principles Board (APB). (If you are interested in getting a sense of FASB's current reform agenda, you should view its website, http://www.fasb.org.)

Another important organization in the field is the American Institute of Certified Public Accountants (AICPA). The AICPA's Auditing Standard Board has traditionally performed a rule-making function in the development of generally accepted auditing standards (GAAS, pronounced like gas). These constitute a separate set of rules that prescribe procedures that outside accountants (also known as independent auditors) are supposed to follow prior to certifying that financial statements comply with GAAP. Mirroring FASB's role in the preparation of statements of accounting standards, the AICPA Audit Board has promulgated rules governing audit practices. For example, the AICPA's Statement on Auditing Standard No. 12 explains how auditors should make inquiries of a client's lawyer concerning litigation, claims, and assessments. (This standard was promulgated in 1975, at the same time that the American Bar Association issued a companion statement of policy for lawyers.) In 2002, in the wake of the widespread scandals in corporate accounting for firms such as Enron and Worldcom, Congress mandated the creation of a new Public Company Accounting Oversight Board to oversee the auditors of public companies, and the Board is likely to have a major impact on the development of auditing standards in the future.

The most broadly based institution involved in the creation of financial statements is the accounting profession itself. At the core of this group are certified public accountants, who are licensed by state accounting boards (analogous to state bar associations for lawyers). To obtain certification as an accountant, a person must pass a test developed under the auspices of the AICPA and satisfy training and apprenticeship requirements, which vary from jurisdiction to jurisdiction. Certified public accountants work in numerous capacities — as corporate employees, most commonly in internal accounting or control departments, as government employees with auditing responsibilities, and as partners or other members of independent accounting firms. The most prominent of the independent accounting firms are the Big Four (formerly the Big Eight): Deloitte & Touche, Ernst & Young, KPMG Peat Marwick, and PricewaterhouseCoopers (doesn't rhyme with anything).

Under SEC regulations, the financial statements of a public company must be audited periodically (usually annually) by an accounting firm that is independent of the company. Typically, the Big Four perform the audits of larger companies. Even firms that are not subject to SEC regulations often choose to subject themselves to independent audits, sometimes to supplement internal controls and other times to establish for third parties, such as creditors, customers, or contributors, the credibility of their financial statements. In many cases, firms are bound by contractual provisions to submit to independent audits annually. In gross numbers, substantially more financial statements are produced each year in response to contractual obligations — that is, private law drafted by attorneys — than as a result of SEC regulations governing public companies. Thus, a final institution responsible for the creation of financial statements in the United States is the legal profession — in other words, you.

The lawyer's perspective

A question that lawyers routinely have to decide is whether, in a given case, to require that financial statements delivered to them be audited by independent auditors. Sometimes they even have to decide whether to specify the kind of accounting firm (i.e., a Big Four firm or some less well known — and presumably less expensive — alternative) that should perform the audit. In reaching their decisions, they must balance the value of obtaining better financial information against the cost of imposing such requirements.

B. Finding Financial Statements and Related Information

The institutional structure outlined above is the engine that generates the financial statements of business organizations and other entities in the United States. And it is this structure that you have to understand in order to locate and use these financial statements and information associated with them. Imagine for a moment that you are a new associate in a law firm and your supervising partner, knowing that you are trained in analytical methods, sticks her head through your office door and says, "I'd like you to check out the financials on Company XYZ." What would you do?

A reasonable first step would be to ask the partner whether the firm is a public company and thus subject to the SEC disclosure and accounting requirements. If she doesn't know, there are a number of ways for you to find out for yourself. One of the simplest is to access the SEC's home page (http://www.sec.gov) and then click on EDGAR Database. (EDGAR, pronounced like the name of the author of *The Telltale Heart,* is an acronym for Electronic Data Gathering, Analysis, and Retrieval; the database contains the filings [i.e., disclosure and accounting documents] of nearly all public companies.) Once there, you can use various search engines and indices to determine whether the firm in question is a public company. If it is, you will have a large amount of financial information about the firm right at your fingertips, usually including its most recent financial statements.

Before we discuss the content of SEC disclosure documents, let's suppose that the partner had told you that the firm was privately owned and thus not subject to SEC regulation. What would you do in this case? A reasonable next question would be, Does Company XYZ have audited financial statements for the preceding year? Because many companies not subject to SEC requirements undergo annual independent audits (either voluntarily or by contractual commitment), independently audited financial statements may indeed be available for Company XYZ, and they may even have been audited by one of the Big Four and therefore be of the same quality as those included in the SEC filings (though not likely to be supplemented with other disclosures that the SEC requires of public companies). If available, these statements would offer valuable insight into the financial posture of Company XYZ.

What if audited financial statements are not available for the company (e.g., if it is family owned and the family has never felt the need to subject the company to an independent audit)? Is there anything else you might ask? One possibility would be to inquire whether the company has any financial statements that were prepared internally. The company would almost certainly generate financial information for its own purposes even if it didn't go to the trouble of having independent audits performed. Though less reliable on numerous dimensions than audited financials, internal statements offer at least some information on the financial status of a company and at times can even be extremely informative.

Let's briefly consider the kind of financial information likely to be found in the various categories of financial statements, starting with the least complete and moving up to SEC disclosure documents.

1. Internal financial statements. The content and quality of internal financial statements are highly variable. In general, we might expect at least the three basic formats (i.e., the balance sheets reporting the firm's year-end financial position for the two most recent years, an income statement for the preceding year or two, and a summary of cash flows for the most recent year), although with smaller firms, all three formats may not be available. We would have no idea about the quality of the statements that are available. The firm may or may not have a CPA on staff; typically, it would not be obligated to. Some other person, who may be marginally trained or even untrained, may be responsible for preparing the documents. Moreover, without investigating further, we could not be certain that the statements fully satisfy GAAP standards, even though they most likely look as if they do. Financial statements do not necessarily conform to even the basic foundational principles that we have addressed, much less the detailed requirements articulated in FASB statements and related lines of authority. There are many reasons why these statements may deviate from GAAP and FASB standards. Perhaps no one on the company's payroll was qualified to prepare them in accordance with GAAP. Or they may have been prepared for a specific purpose where full GAAP compliance may not have seemed necessary — such as calculating bonuses for the sales staff. Another possibility is that they had been put together to show low income for tax purposes. What's more, internal financial statements do not necessarily fully reflect all or even most of the firm's economic activities. For example, we cannot possibly know, simply by looking at an internal balance sheet, if all of the company's liabilities appear on it.

2. Audited financial statements. Considering the limitations of and uncertainties about internally generated financial statements, the advantages of ones audited by independent accounting firms are obvious. Hiring an independent auditor is supposed to ensure quality, and this assurance is expressed formally in the auditor's report that accompanies audited financials.

A typical auditor's report appears in Box 3. This report is from audited financial statements appended to the 2001 Financial Report of Outback Steakhouses, Inc. (The company's 2002 Financial Report is appended to this chapter). If you look at it carefully,

---

Box 3
Report of Independent Accountants

To the Board of Directors and
Stockholders of Outback Steakhouse, Inc.

In our opinion, the accompanying consolidated balance sheets and the related consolidated statements of income, stockholders' equity and cash flows present fairly, in all material respects, the financial position of Outback Steakhouse, Inc. (the "Company") at December 21, 2001 and 2000, and the results of their operations and their cash flows for each of the three years in the period ended December 21, 2001, in conformity with accounting principles generally accepted in the United States of America. These financial statements are the responsibility of the Company's management; our responsibility is to express an opinion on these financial statements based on our audits. We conducted our audits of these statements in accordance with auditing standards generally accepted in the United States of America, which require that we plan and perform the audit to obtain reasonable assurance about whether the financial statements are free of material misstatement. An audit includes examining, on a test basis, evidence supporting the amounts and disclosures in the financial statements, assessing the accounting principles used and significant estimates made by management, and evaluating the overall financial statement presentation. We believe that our audits provide a reasonable basis for our opinion.

PriceWaterhouseCoopers LLP
February 12, 2002

---

you will note that a number of statements speak to the quality of the financials and explain how they were prepared.

First, notice to whom the report is addressed: the Board of the Directors and Stockholders of Outback Steakhouse. What's going on in the report is that the independent accountant — PricewaterhouseCoopers, one of the Big Four — is reporting to these parties about Outback Steakhouse's financial statements for the period 2000-2001.

Second, the bottom line of the opinion (in the first sentence of text) is that the financial statements attached to the auditor's report "present fairly, in all material respects" the company's financial position "in conformity with *generally accepted accounting principles.*" With this sentence, the independent auditor assures the members of the Board and anyone else who reads the report not just that the structure of the statements complies with the FASB rules but also that the statements are supplemented with appropriate footnotes and additional information that GAAP requires. (If you look at the Outback Steakhouse 2002 Financial Report appended to this chapter, you'll see that the three basic formats take up only a few pages starting on page 142, whereas the footnotes and supplemental statements run for a few dozen pages. Note 11 on pages 156-157, for example, discusses litigation and was almost certainly drafted with the assistance of attorneys.)

Third, the report speaks to the auditor's confidence that the financial statements do, in fact, reflect all of the firm's economic activity during the relevant periods. Importantly, the auditor does not claim to have comprehensively reviewed all of the firm's activities. Even with audited financials, the actual preparation of financial statements remains the responsibility of management and is usually undertaken by CPAs and support staff. The auditor purports to have conducted the audit of those financial statements in accordance with generally accepted auditing standards (GAAS), the rules developed under the auspices of the AICPA's Audit Board. As explained in the report, the independent auditor simply spot-checked (i.e., "examin[ed], on a test basis") the company's internal procedures as well as the accounting standards and estimates used to compile the financial statements. These procedures are designed to provide the auditor with a "reasonable basis" for the opinion, as expressed in the first sentence, that the financial statements are a materially fair presentation of the company's financial position in accordance with GAAP. This assurance may strike you as cramped and legalistic, but it is substantially more reassuring than what typically accompanies unaudited, internally generated financial statements.

3. Financial statements of public companies. The gold standard of financial disclosure in the United States can be seen in the financial statements of public corporations — firms subject to the SEC rules governing disclosure and financial statements. The details of SEC-mandated disclosure are well beyond our scope. But to get a sense of the kinds of additional financial information that public companies in the United States must provide, you should flip through the Outback Steakhouse Financial Report (appended to this chapter). Although the company is relatively small and has a narrow range of business activities, the document contains a number of interesting features that exemplify disclosure required by the SEC:

- The SEC mandates that all public firms have their financial statements audited by independent accounting firms in accordance with GAAS, with respect to financial statements maintained in accordance with GAAP. (Actually, the SEC accounting rules go beyond GAAP in several respects, but this subject is beyond the scope of our coverage.)

- The SEC requires public firms to disclose a great deal of information in addition to that in their audited financial statements. This information, much of which is financial, must be included in their SEC filings. For example, they include a textual description of a firm's financial statements accompanied by a discussion of trends and future prospects, which financial analysts read with great care. (An example of this can be seen in the Management's Discussion and Analysis of Financial Condition and Results of Operation, which appears at the front of the the Outback Steakhouse Financial Report.) Lawyers often have a role in drafting this kind of disclosure as well as related sections on cautionary statements (see, e.g., pages 139-140). A list of the firm's major contracts and documents that can be retrieved from other sources may also appear in the SEC filing.

- The legal regimen surrounding documents filed with the SEC is much more stringent than generally applicable legal rules or even the rules governing financial statements of nonpublic companies. This is especially true when the documents are used in connection with the public sale of securities. For this reason, companies, their accountants, and other advisers are extremely careful in preparing SEC disclosure documents. The quality of the information in these filings is thus typically quite high.

4. Qualified auditors' reports. At this stage, a note of warning is in order about another feature of auditors' reports: whether or not they contain qualifications. The report in Box 3 is what's known as an *unqualified report*. The auditor didn't find it necessary to include any qualifying statement. This is the kind of a report that a firm wants to get and analysts expect to see. On occasion, however, an auditor's report can be *qualified* in one or more respects. Any qualification should be evaluated carefully. Examples

> **Box 4**
> **Excerpt from the E. I. du Pont de Nemours**
> **and Company Annual Report of 1994**
>
> . . . We believe that our audits provide a reasonable basis for our opinion.
>
> As discussed in Note 1 to the consolidated financial statements, the company changed its method of accounting for postretirement benefits other than pensions and for income taxes in 1992.

of qualifying language can be seen in the excerpts from audit letters in Boxes 4, 5, and 6.

Sometimes qualifications are fairly technical. For instance, in Box 4, we see that du Pont changed the way in which it accounted for certain kinds of retirement benefits during the period covered by the report. This change was, in fact, mandated by the release of a new FASB standard, but it had an impact at several places in the firm's statement, and the qualification was intended to alert readers to this fact. The Outback Steakhouse 2002 Financial Report has a comparable qualification. What does it concern? (See page 163.)

The qualification in the report in Box 5 is the sort that often appears in audit reports prepared by foreign issuers — in this case, the Irish Telephone Company. The auditor includes the qualification that the financials were prepared in accordance with Irish GAAP, not U.S. GAAP. One of the principal differences — that Irish GAAP permits some assets to be valued at depreciated replacement cost as opposed to depreciated historical cost — is explained, and readers are directed to note 33 for a more detailed explanation of the differences between the two accounting treatments. In essence, this type of qualification is a warning that the financials deviate from U.S. GAAP in a way that the SEC sometimes permits for certain foreign companies.

The most serious qualification appears in the report in Box 6. In the first paragraph, the accountant raises a "going concern"

Box 5
Excerpt from the Prospectus
of Telecom Eireann, July 7, 1999

. . . In our opinion, the consolidated financial statements referred to above present fairly, in all material respects, the consolidated financial position of Bord Telecom Eireann ple and subsidiaries as at 3 April 1997, 2 April 1998 and 1 April 1999, and the consolidated results of their operations, cash flows and changes in equity shareholders' funds for each of the three years in the period ended 1 April 1999, in conformity with *generally accepted accounting principles in Ireland* [italics added].

Generally accepted accounting principles in Ireland vary in certain significant respects from accounting principles generally accepted in the United States of America ("US GAAP"). The application of the latter would have affected the determination of consolidated results for each of the two years in the period ended 1 April 1999 and equity shareholders' funds as at 2 April 1998 and 1 April 1999 to the extent summarized in Note 33 to the consolidated financial statements. As described in Note 33, certain tangible assets were recorded at depreciated replacement cost at the start of business of Bord Telecom Eireann ple on 1 January 1984, in accordance with the Postal and Telecommunication Services Act, 1983, rather than their historical cost, as required by US GAAP.

---

qualification. In light of the firm's current and pending financial commitments, the auditors raise substantial doubt about the firm's ability to continue operating. This doubt, in effect, precludes the issuance of a clean opinion because GAAP is based on the assumption that the reporting entity will continue operations — a point emphasized in the first sentence of the excerpt. A qualification of this sort is a flashing red light in the world of financial accounting. A second sort of qualification — one concerning the reasonableness of management's estimates of losses from out-

Box 6
Excerpt from the Knudsen Corporation
Annual Report of 1995

The accompanying consolidated financial statements have been prepared assuming that the Corporation will continue as a going concern. As discussed in "Notes to Consolidated Financial Statements – Basis of Presentation and Management's Plans," the Corporation had substantial losses and negative cash flow from operations in 1994, which significantly reduced stockholders' equity and resulted in a substantial retained deficit and working capital deficit at December 31, 1994; was not in compliance with certain financial covenants of certain of its credit agreements at December 31, 1994 and subsequently failed to meet scheduled repayment terms; and will require additional funding to cover substantial expected negative cash flows in 1995. In addition, substantially all of the of the Corporation's short-term debt agreements expire on July 31, 1995. If the Corporation is unable to obtain adequate financing, it may be required to seek protection under the United States Bankruptcy Code in order to continue operating. *These conditions raise substantial doubt about the Corporation's ability to continue as a going concern* [italics added]. Management's plans in this regard are also described in the "Notes to Consolidated Financial Statements – Basis of Presentation and Management's Plans." The consolidated financial statements do not include any adjustments that might result from the outcome of this uncertainty.

As emphasized in "Notes to Consolidated Financial Statements – Estimated Losses on Uncompleted Contracts," the Corporation recorded significant provisions for losses during 1994 related to revised estimates of costs to be incurred to complete certain transit car contracts. *These management estimates are based on numerous assumptions which, if not ultimately achieved, could result in additional revisions of the estimates of costs to complete the transit car contracts and such revisions could be material* [italics added].

standing contractual obligations — is raised in the second paragraph of Box 6. Most analysts would be concerned by this qualification and would want to investigate its implications.

6. The Analysis of Financial Statements

Knowing how to create financial statements is one thing. Being able to assess the information in them is yet another. For example, in looking back at the income statement in Figure 3, we see that the firm's net income was $718,200. But how do we evaluate this figure? Did the company do worse than one that made more than $1 million during the same period? Better than one that made only $500,000? Can we, in fact, answer these questions without having additional information? (Answer: No, we need more information.)

Evaluating financial statements is a discipline unto itself. In business schools, entire courses are devoted to the analysis of corporate financial reports, and financial analysts make their living helping investors decipher the periodic disclosures of public companies. Analysts have a wide variety of techniques (including many financial techniques that the next chapter addresses) at their disposal. *Ratio analysis* is an important one. It focuses attention on the relationship between various components of a firm's financial statements. Each ratio provides a certain kind of information when assessing a company. Analysts look at each ratio to determine whether it falls within a range appropriate for that firm. If it falls outside the benchmark range that has been established as the norm, additional investigation may be in order.

Applying ratio analysis necessitates revisiting the basic components of financial statements and reviewing the relationships among the components. Let's take a look at some basic financial ratios. The limitations of ratio analysis — dependent as it is on financial statements built on accounting conventions such as historical costs — offer an appropriate springboard for the more sophisticated methodologies of finance that are addressed in the next chapter.

The lawyer's perspective

When the line between legal and financial advice blurs, as it often does, lawyers are at an advantage if they understand financial ratios. But even an attorney working in an entirely legal context must occasionally make use of financial ratios. Loan covenants, for example, often include restrictions that require the borrower to maintain one or more of these ratios within a certain range. Failure to do so can constitute default —and is often defined as such in contracts — with economic consequences that can be dire for the borrower. To be able to draft such provisions or offer advice about them, an attorney must understand their significance.

A. Liquidity

One way to assess liquidity is to determine how much cash or cash reserves an individual or entity has on hand at a given time. You can obtain this information by looking at the entity's balance sheet. Alternatively, you could inspect the summary of cash flows to see how cash reserves have changed over time. Taking yet another approach, you could look at the firm's current ratio, which is the ratio of its current assets (i.e., the sum of cash and assets likely to be converted into cash in the near future) to its current (or short-term) liabilities. Analysts track this ratio because, intuitively, current assets should always be greater than short-term liabilities. Indeed, as a rule of thumb, the current ratio should always be greater than 1.5 to 2.0 — that is, current assets should be at least one and a half to two times as large as current liabilities.

To test your understanding of how the current ratio is calculated, look back at Figures 1 and 2. Do you see why that firm's current ratio is expressed by the following equation?

$$\text{current ratio} = \frac{\text{current assets}}{\text{current liabilities}}$$

$$= \frac{\$3,415,807}{\$1,546,107}$$

$$\approx 2.21$$

Note that the calculated current ratio is larger than the bench-mark (1.5 to 2.0) that was just mentioned. In other words, the firm's liquidity is within acceptable bounds, though taking on a large amount of new short-term debt may not be prudent. How might the firm improve its current ratio, thereby making itself more attractive to short-term creditors?

B. Solvency

In a similar spirit, other financial ratios test a firm's solvency. Analysts approach solvency from two perspectives. One is by considering the ratio between a firm's liabilities and other com-ponents of its balance sheets. The measures most commonly looked at are the ratio of debt to equity and the related ratio of debt to total assets. The intuition here is that if a firm has too much debt (in financial parlance, is too highly leveraged), its sol-vency is imperiled: even a slight downturn in profitability could leave the firm incapable of repaying its creditors.

Criteria for evaluating leverage ratios vary considerably from industry to industry. The financial services industry tends to be highly leveraged, with debt equivalent to more than 90% of as-sets — that is, a debt-to-equity ratio of more than 9 to 1. The ratio tends to be much lower for manufacturing firms. For example, the total liabilities of the hypothetical firm we considered earlier were $2,296,107 (i.e., current liabilities of $1,546,107 plus long-term notes of $750,000), and its total owners' equity was $3,319,700. So its debt-to-equity ratio was 0.69 — in other words, its total liabilities were roughly equal to two-thirds of its total owners' equity. Measured against its total assets ($5,615,807), its debt was about 40.9%. One interpretation of this figure is that, for every dollar of assets, the firm financed about 41 cents with debt and the other 59 cents with owners' money. All in all, these are considered to be relatively conservative leverage ratios.

The second way that analysts quantify solvency is by compar-ing a firm's annual interest expenses to the earnings it has available to make these payments. By convention, this is a comparison of earnings before interest and tax (EBIT, rhymes with rivet) to annual interest expense.[1] (In the income statement in Figure 3, EBIT is called *operating earnings*.) This ratio is sometimes called ~~interest coverage~~, and the larger this figure is, the more likely the firm is to be able to pay its future interest obligations as they come due. For example, if the ratio of EBIT to interest expense for a firm were 10 to 1, it could continue to make its interest payments even if its earnings declined by 90%. Do you see why? As an exercise, try to calculate the interest coverage ratio for our hypothetical firm. (Answer: 12.62.)

C. Managerial Efficiency

A number of ratios relate to the efficiency of a firm's management. For example, sometimes analysts are interested in the relationship between a firm's accounts receivables and its gross revenues. The intuition here is that accounts receivable (i.e., the total amount of customer bills outstanding) should not be too great relative to the firm's annual sales. If too many customers aren't paying their bills, that's a bad sign. So, all other things being equal, when a firm's accounts receivable are more than 15% of its annual revenues, eyebrows might rise, particularly if the ratio is higher than it had been in the past.

Looking back to Figures 1 and 3, confirm that the ratio of accounts receivable to sales revenue would be roughly 10%:

$$\frac{\text{accounts receivable}}{\text{sales revenue}} = \frac{\$1,000,000}{\$10,400,000}$$

$$\approx 0.096$$

---

1. The logic for using a measure of income that does not include interest or taxes is as follows: As to interest, because we are trying to figure out the earnings available to pay interest, interest should not already have been deducted from the amount of earnings available to pay interest. As to taxes, the theory is that taxes are due only on net income, so tax is paid only on the earnings remaining after interest has been paid. The obligation to pay interest, in this sense, has precedence over the obligation to pay taxes. In the extreme case, if EBIT equaled $100 and interest payments equaled $100, the firm would have no income for the period in question, and no taxes would be due.

If we assumed that sales revenue had been generated evenly throughout the year, we would see that customers had been taking 5 weeks, on average, to pay off their accounts (i.e., 0.096 × 52 weeks = 4.99 weeks). This would usually be considered a reasonable period.

Many other ratios are used to measure managerial performance. One of these is the *turnover ratio* — that is, the ratio of cost of goods sold to year-end inventory. It is an estimate of how many times a firm's inventory is sold during a year. The higher the turnover ratio, the more efficient the firm's inventory management is, or, in other words, the shorter the period of time items stay in inventory, the lower the firm's cost of maintaining inventory is. Among other useful ratios are those that relate interest payments to debt (providing a measure of a firm's interest costs) and after-tax income to pre-tax income (a measure of a firm's tax rate). Many other kinds of performance measures are possible. Measures of this sort are often used to evaluate the performance of individual employees, and they can even be used to calculate compensation packages.

D. Profitability

Another set of performance measures look to a firm's profitability. Again, this issue can be approached from a variety of perspectives, and relevant benchmarks vary considerably from industry to industry. For example, we could look at the ratio of a firm's operating earnings to its sales revenue, also referred to as the firm's *margin.* This ratio reflects the percentage of sales that remained after direct costs (costs of goods sold) and indirect costs (operating expenses) were deducted. If we look at Figure 3 and calculate the margin from information in the income statement there, we find that it's 12.5%: $1,300,000/$10,400,000 = 0.125 (i.e., operating income/sales revenue). So, for this firm, every dollar of sales generated 12.5 cents of operating income. Supermarkets typically have much thinner (lower) margins, whereas high-tech firms like Microsoft have much higher ones.

Another way to approach profitability is to compare earnings to the total amount of money invested in a firm. Ratios of this sort explore the relationship between income and balance sheet entries. By convention, the measure of income typically used is *net income* — that is, operating earnings minus interest expenses and taxes.[2] On the balance sheet side, total assets and total owners' equity are the entries used most often. The ratio of net income to total assets is the *return on assets* (ROA), which we can think of as the amount of income that each dollar of assets generated during the reporting period. Look back at Figures 1 and 3 and try to locate the components of the following equation:

$$\text{return on assets} = \frac{\text{net income}}{\text{total assets}}$$
$$= \frac{\$718,200}{\$5,615,807}$$
$$\approx 12.79\%$$

The other common measure of profitability compares net income to owners' equity. This ratio, the *return on equity* (ROE), is, in effect, a measure of the return on the owners' investment in a firm. In our hypothetical firm, it would be calculated as follows:

$$\text{return on equity} = \frac{\text{net income}}{\text{total owners' equity}}$$
$$= \frac{\$718,200}{\$3,319,700}$$
$$\approx 21.63\%$$

For this hypothetical firm, the ROE (21.63%) is higher than its ROA (12.79%). Intuitively, this makes sense because owners' equity was less than total assets. And owners' equity was less than total assets because the firm had leveraged its equity with a certain amount of debt (in fact, about 69 cents of debt for every dol-

---

2. The reason for using a more complete measure of earnings in this context is that the ratios at issue here — ROA and ROE — are intended to provide something of a bottom line on a firm's profitability. Net income is appropriate for such applications because it presents the fullest picture of a firm's earnings.

lar of equity; see the discussion of solvency). For a firm that has no liabilities — that is, one that is fully funded with equity — ROA equals ROE. Do you see why? No Leverage

E. Earnings per Share and Price-Earnings Ratios

This final category of measurements offers ways to relate accounting statement measures of profitability to a more ephemeral concept: market values. Recall that throughout our discussion of financial analysis we have been working with components of financial statements that, under GAAP, are principally based on historical costs. There is no guarantee that accounting entries on accounting statements will accord with market values. So, for example, if we were interested in estimating the market value of a company or a share of stock in this company (which constitutes a pro rata interest in the firm), turning to the firm's financial statements will be of only limited use. The component of the balance sheet that most closely accords with the value of the firm is total owners' equity ($3,319,807 for our hypothetical firm). If this number is divided by the number of shares of stock outstanding, we can calculate a *book value* for a share of stock: $16.60 (i.e., total owners' equity/number of shares of common stock outstanding = $3,319,807/200,000 shares = $16.60 per share).

But a book value may or may not be a good estimate of the true market value of a firm or its shares. As we saw earlier, financial statements are built on historical costs, which do not reflect appreciation or deterioration in the value of certain long-lived assets. Moreover, the value of many intangible assets (e.g., reputation, employee morale, intellectual property) may not be reflected in financial statements. Finally, various contingencies that are difficult to place a value on (e.g., lawsuits) may not be reflected in the book value of owners' equity. In the case of Microsoft, for example, the government's antitrust suit wouldn't have appeared on its balance sheet (although it would presumably have been discussed in the notes to the company's financial statements.)

Many of these shortcomings are inherent in the nature of financial statements and cannot easily be avoided without resorting to wholly different valuation techniques (such as financial economics). But analysts do have one or two measures that may be more useful than simple calculations of book value per share.

One of these — *earnings per share* (EPS) — compares net income to number of shares outstanding. It is a measurement of the amount of earnings attributable to each share. Our hypothetical firm reported a net income of $718,200 (see Figure 3) and 200,000 shares of common stock outstanding (capital stock in Figure 2). Hence, its EPS was $3.56. This ratio is often used to evaluate the market price of a company's stock. For example, if you were trying to determine how much you would be willing to pay for a share of stock, you might ask yourself how much you would be willing to pay in order to receive $3.56 of income a year from a company of this sort. If we thought this income stream would continue indefinitely and expected a 10% return on this sort of investment, we might be willing to pay $35.60 per share (i.e., $3.56 is 10% of $35.60). Note that this is more than twice as much as the firm's book value per share ($16.60). Such discrepancy reinforces the point that market values may well deviate from book values.

A related ratio compares a firm's EPS to the actual market value of the firm's stock. Because this measure relies on market values, it can be calculated only for companies whose securities trade in the public markets or otherwise have a readily obtainable market price. In the United States, this information is generally available only for public firms that are subject to SEC regulations for disclosure, such as Outback Steakhouses. The standard way of expressing the relationship of market value to EPS is by calculating the ratio of the price of a firm's common stock to the earnings per share of the stock. This ratio is the *price-earnings multiple,* sometimes referred to as the *PE ratio.* If you flip through the Outback Steakhouse 2002 Financial Report, you can see that the company's basic EPS in 2002 was $2.04 (see page 143). In the fourth quarter of 2002, its stock price ranged from $24.90 to $36.09 per share (see page 164). Dividing the midpoint of this trading range ($30.49) by the 2002 EPS yields a PE ratio of 14.95. In the past, such a ratio would have been considered reasonably high. In the market of the late 1990s, however, where high-tech startups were favored investments, much higher multiples were reported. In fact, PE ratios greater than 100 were not uncommon. Should this have been a warning sign to financial analysts?

7. Suggestions for Further Reading

If you're interested in learning more about accounting, you can find additional information in the publications listed below. A number of the topics addressed in the next chapter (Finance) build on the accounting principles and techniques that we have just worked through.

Robert N. Anthony, *Essentials of Accounting,* 8th ed. (Reading, MA: Addison-Wesley Publishing Company, 2002).

Lawrence A. Cunningham, *Introductory Accounting and Finance for Lawyers,* 3rd ed. (St. Paul, MN : West Group, 2002).

David R. Herwitz and Matthew J. Barrett, *Accounting for Lawyers,* 3rd ed. (Westbury, NY : Foundation Press, 2001).

Gary John Previts and Barbara Dubis Merino, *A History of Accountancy in the United States: The Cultural Significance of Accounting* (Columbus, OH : Ohio State University Press, 1998).

Howard M. Schilit, *Financial Shenanigans: How to Detect Accounting Gimmicks and Fraud in Financial Reports,* 2nd ed. (Boston, MA : McGraw-Hill, 2002).

John A. Tracy, *How to Read a Financial Report: For Managers, Entrepreneurs, Lenders, Lawyers, and Investors,* 5th ed. (New York, NY : John Wiley & Sons, Inc., 1999).

Gerald I. White et al., *The Analysis and Use of Financial Statements,* 2d ed. (New York, NY : John Wiley & Sons, Inc., 1997).

Finance

1. Introduction

What is finance? To many, the term conjures up phalanxes of well-heeled investment bankers and gargantuan sums of money whizzing back and forth across international borders. To be sure, these caricatures reflect facets of the world of finance. But finance is also an academic discipline — less glamorous than the Wall Street of Hollywood imaginations, but a field of study with its own logic and organizing principles. The contours of the field are not always clear, but one leading text offers the following definition:

> Finance is the study of how people allocate scarce resources *over time*. Two features that distinguish financial decisions from other resource allocation decisions are that the costs and benefits of financial decisions are (1) spread out over time and (2) usually not known with certainty in advance by either the decision maker or anybody else.[3]

As a rough cut, this synopsis is quite helpful. First, it highlights the inter-temporal dimension of the subject. The techniques we will be studying in this chapter are designed to balance the costs of taking some action today — making an investment or entering into a contract — with benefits that will accrue from that action at some time in the future — as a stream of dividends or some other form of return. Second, the definition emphasizes a critical dimension of financial analysis: problems of finance almost always involve uncertainty. When deciding whether to purchase shares in a particular company, an investor does not know — is

---

3. Zvi Bodie & Robert C. Merton, *Finance* 2 (1999).

uncertain — whether the firm will turn out to be a dud or the next Microsoft. When a university is offered the opportunity to purchase a piece of land, it cannot know for certain whether another, more attractive piece of land might become available tomorrow. Finance provides a set of tools for evaluating these uncertainties.

Another important preliminary point to recognize about the field of finance is its recent pedigree. Unlike accounting, whose roots can be traced back over five hundred years, the study of finance is comparatively new. Although the foundations of financial theory were laid in a smattering of academic papers in the 1930s, real progress in the field did not begin until the post–World War II era. Works that now stand as seminal contributions date back only to the 1950s and early 1960s, and the first Nobel Prizes for work in the field were not awarded until the 1990s.[4] So the field of finance is still new and evolving rapidly.

Finally, the field of finance can be extraordinarily complex. The theoretical arguments upon which modern finance is based are often elaborate and multifaceted. Moreover, much of the debate over financial theory turns upon the interpretation of empirical evidence accumulated and presented through the use of econometric analysis (akin to the techniques that we introduced in the chapters on statistics and regression analysis in *Analytical Methods for Lawyers*). Unlike issues of accounting, which often can be

---

4. The first prize, awarded in 1990, went to Harry Markowitz (for work on portfolio theory), William Sharp (for developing the capital asset pricing model), and Merton Miller (for contributions to the theory of corporate finance). The 1997 Nobel Prize was shared by Robert C. Merton and Myron Scholes for their contribution to options pricing theory. By the end of this chapter, you should have at least a general sense of the nature of the academic achievements of these individuals. Two other authors whose work is excerpted in this chapter also won Nobel Prizes in economics but not for work that would ordinarily be characterized as pure finance: Franco Modigliani in 1985 for his work on the analysis of savings and of financial markets and Ronald Coase in 1991 for his work on transaction costs and property rights.

reduced to addition, subtraction, multiplication, and occasionally division, financial arguments routinely employ calculus and other sorts of higher-level mathematics. With finance, sooner or later everyone is in over his or her head.

Nevertheless, finance is a field with which attorneys must have some familiarity. Most obviously, corporate counsel must comprehend the logic of finance because many business transactions are designed to advance financial goals and because associated documentation and negotiations must comport with the transactions' purposes. But financial considerations are relevant to a much broader category of lawyers. Attorneys practicing family law spend much of their time on estate planning and marital disputes, areas where uncertain costs and benefits must be balanced over time — that is, areas well suited to financial analysis. Indeed, one could plausibly argue that in every area of law in which decision analysis might be applied (this includes litigation, negotiations, and many other areas of legal practice), a lawyer might make use of financial techniques to establish appropriate endpoint values. For example, when considering the value of going to trial, an attorney is evaluating the likelihood of success (an uncertainty) at the end of a trial (a point in the future). In fact, one could think of finance as a specialized extension of decision analysis, where the mechanical elements of the decision trees are superseded by more efficient (but less transparent) analytical tools.

Within the confines of this chapter, we will not be able to address the tools of finance in any detail, but we will attempt to give an overview of a number of analytical methods that make use of financial theory and that a broad range of attorneys routinely encounter or employ. We will begin with several qualitative — as opposed to technical — financial arguments employed in legal analysis and featured prominently in upper-level law school courses, including Corporations and Taxation. Next we will present a number of important financial techniques and theories: the time value of money, the basic principles of portfolio diversification, the risk-return trade-off, the efficient market hypothesis, and the capital asset pricing model. We will complete the chapter with an introduction of valuation techniques that financial analysts and other business people typically use to appraise financial assets and investment opportunities.

2. The Foundations of Financial Theory

To introduce the subject of finance, we begin with a selection of excerpts from important academic papers in the field. Our goal in presenting these readings is twofold. First, these excerpts illustrate the intellectual underpinnings of the discipline, both illuminating the kinds of problems financial analysis was developed to solve and suggesting the basic logic of finance. Second, this section introduces students to several of the most prominent thinkers in the field. In upper-level law school courses and sometimes even in the world of practice, reference will be made to *Coasean analysis* or a *Berle and Means corporation* or the *Modigliani and Miller theorem*. Well-trained lawyers should have at least a passing familiarity with these intellectual landmarks.

A. The Theory of the Firm

The theory of the firm was one of the first problems that attracted the attention of financial theorists. In this area, economists strive to understand the economic function of firms. We start with what may be the most famous and frequently cited article on the subject. Here, Nobel laureate Ronald Coase (to whom you may have been introduced in other first-year courses) addresses the question of why some economic activities are located within a firm while other activities are organized through transactions executed at prices determined by the market — that is, through contracts. The answer offered in this excerpt has had a major impact on the field of finance as well as other areas of economic study.

R. H. Coase
The Nature of the Firm
4 *Economica* 386, 389–93 (1937)

[T]he distinguishing mark of the firm is the supersession of the price mechanism. . . .

Our task is to attempt to discover why a firm emerges at all in a specialized exchange economy. . . .

The main reason why it is profitable to establish a firm would seem to be that there is a cost of using the price mechanism. The most obvious cost of "organizing" production through the price mechanism is that of discovering what relevant prices are. This cost may be reduced but it will not be eliminated by the emergence of specialists who will sell this information. The costs of negotiating and concluding a separate contract for each exchange transaction which takes place on a market must also be taken into account . . . It is true that contracts are not eliminated when there is a firm but they are greatly reduced. A factor of production (or the owner thereof) does not have to make a series of contracts with the factors with whom he is co-operating within the firm, as would be necessary, of course, if this co-operation were as a direct result of the working of the price mechanism. For this series of contracts is substituted one. At this stage, it is important to note the character of the contract into which a factor enters that is employed within a firm. The contract is one whereby the factor, for a certain remuneration (which can be fixed or fluctuating) agrees to obey the directions of an entrepreneur *within certain limits.* The essence of the contract is that it should only state the limits to the powers of the entrepreneur. Within these limits, he can therefore direct the other factors of production.

There are, however, other disadvantages — or costs — of using the price mechanism. It may be desired to make a long-term contract for the supply of some article or service. This may be due to the fact that if one contract is made for a longer period, instead of several shorter ones, then certain costs of making each contract will be avoided. Or, owing to the risk attitude of the people concerned, they may prefer to make a long rather than a short-term contract. Now, owing to the difficulty of forecasting, the longer the period of the contract is for the supply of the commodity or service, the less possible, and indeed, the less desirable it is for the person purchasing to specify what the other contracting party is expected to do. It may well be a matter of indifference to the person supplying the service or commodity which of several courses of action is taken, but not to the purchaser of that service or commodity. But the purchaser will not know which of these several courses he will want the supplier to take. Therefore the service which is being provided is expressed in general terms, the exact details being left until a later date. All that is stated in the contract is the limits to what the persons supplying the commodity or service is expected to do. The details of what the supplier is expected to do is not stated in the contract but is decided later by the purchaser. When the direction of resources (within the limits of the contract) becomes dependent on the buyer in this way, that relationship which I term a "firm" may be obtained. A firm is therefore likely to emerge in those cases where a very short term contract would be unsatisfactory. . . .

We may sum up this section of the argument by saying that the operation of a market costs something and by forming an organization and allowing some authority (an "entrepreneur") to direct the resources, certain marketing costs are saved. The entrepreneur has to carry out his function at less cost, taking into account the fact that he may get factors of production at a lower price than the market transactions which he supersedes, because it is always possible to revert to the open market if he fails to do this.

The question of uncertainty is one which is often considered to be very relevant to the study of the equilibrium of the firm. It seems improbable that a firm would emerge without the existence of uncertainty. . . .

> Another factor that should be noted is that the exchange transactions on a market and the same transactions organized within a firm are often treated differently by Governments or other bodies with regulatory powers. . . .
>
> These, then, are the reasons why organizations such as firms exist in a specialized exchange economy in which it is generally assumed that the distribution of resources is "organized" by the price mechanism. A firm, therefore, consists of the system of relationships which comes into existence when the direction of resources is dependent on an entrepreneur.

This excerpt may strike some students as familiar. The question it considers — under what circumstances is economic activity located within the firm? — is really the inverse of one of the principal questions we would consider in contracting: When should a party (including a firm) use contractual arrangements to farm out a project? Indeed, Professor Coase's definition of a firm is an organization within which economic activity is centralized under the discretionary authority of an entrepreneur. Professor Coase's paper has had a major influence on the way we now think and talk about the organization of economic activity.

But there is also an important practical legacy of Professor Coase's *Nature of the Firm:* the notion that corporate managers and owners must constantly be on the lookout for opportunities to reduce costs and increase efficiencies by moving certain economic activities into or outside a particular firm. Mergers and acquisitions (the aggregation of economic functions) and corporate downsizing (the divestiture of activities) are staples of corporate finance. One way of understanding the role of the phalanxes of investment bankers and management consultants deployed across the American economic landscape is that these individuals are in the business of rationalizing the structure of American business in precisely the manner Professor Coase outlined above. And, of course, the ranks of lawyers who service these financial professionals are also playing an important role in this enterprise.

Another important point to note about the excerpt from Professor Coase's article is the role he assigns to entrepreneurial discretion. One of the reasons it makes sense to move economic activity into the firm is the value of allowing the firm's managers the latitude to organize firm resources as opportunities arise — to assign workers to different tasks or deploy equipment in new ways. This discretion, according to Coase, is what distinguishes the firm from market transactions.[5] As you will see when you study corporate law, the preservation of managerial discretion is one of the hallmarks of American corporate law. Practicing lawyers must also be constantly mindful of the problems created when contractual commitments or legislative reforms threaten to infringe upon managerial discretion. Oftentimes, lawyers must take on the role of explaining why it is important for managers to retain the freedom to manage. Advocacy in this vein often draws upon the contributions of Professor Coase and his successors.

With discretion, however, comes the potential for abuse. This was true in the context of contracting, and it is also true with respect to the theory of the firm. The classic treatment of the less savory side of managerial discretion was published just a few years before Professor Coase's article in a famous book written by two Columbia University professors, Adolf Berle of Columbia Law School and Gardiner Means of the Columbia Economics Department.

---

5. Having studied contracting, some students may recognize that Professor Coase's distinction between inflexible contractual arrangements and discretionary allocations of resources within the structure of a firm is overstated. There are many ways to write contracts to give additional discretion to particular parties, that is, to make the contractual relationship more firmlike. Conversely, modern corporate law scholars increasingly discuss corporate law in contractarian terms, emphasizing that corporate charters can best be understood as specialized forms of contracts. These developments in legal thinking in no way diminish the importance of Professor Coase's original insight. By articulating fundamental distinctions between firms and market transactions, he contributed to intellectual developments that changed the way we think about both fields.

Adolf A. Berle and Gardiner C. Means
The Modern Corporation and Private Property
Chapter 1 (1932)

Corporations have ceased to be merely legal devices through which the private business transactions of individuals may be carried on. Though still much used for this purpose, the corporate form has acquired a larger significance. The corporation has, in fact, become both a method of property tenure and a means of organizing economic life. Grown to tremendous proportions, there may be said to have evolved a "corporate system" — as there was once a feudal system — which has attracted to itself a combination of attributes and powers, and has attained a degree of prominence entitling it to be dealt with as a major social institution. . . .

In its new aspect the corporation is a means whereby the wealth of innumerable individuals has been concentrated into huge aggregates and whereby control over this wealth has been surrendered to a unified direction. The power attendant upon such concentration has brought forth princes of industry, whose position in the community is yet to be defined. The surrender of control over their wealth by investors has effectively broken the old property relationships and has raised the problem of defining these relationships anew. The direction of industry by persons other than those who have ventured their wealth has raised the question of the motive force back of such direction and the effective distribution of the returns from business enterprise. . . .

Such organization of economic activity rests on two developments, each of which has made possible an extension of the area under unified control. The factory system, the basis of the industrial revolution, brought an increasingly large number of workers directly under a single management. Then, the modern corporation, equally revolutionary in its effect, placed the wealth of innumerable individuals under the same central control. By each of these changes the power of those in control was immensely enlarged and the status of those involved, worker or property owner, was radically changed. The independent worker who entered the factory became a wage laborer surrendering the direction of his labor to his industrial master. The property owner who invests in a modern corporation so far surrenders his wealth to those in control of the corporation that he has exchanged the position of independent owner for one in which he may become merely recipient of the wages of capital.

In and of itself, the corporate device does not necessarily bring about this change. It has long been possible for an individual to incorporate his business even though it still represents his own investment, his own activities, and his own business transactions; he has in fact merely created a legal alter ego by setting up a corporation as the nominal vehicle. If the corporate form had done nothing more than this, we should have only an interesting custom according to which business was carried on by individuals adopting for that purpose certain legal clothing. It would involve no radical shift in property tenure or in the organization of economic activity; it would inaugurate no "system" compared to the institutions of feudalism.

The corporate system appears only when this type of private or "close" corporation has given way to an essentially different form, the quasi-public corporation: a corporation in which a large measure of separation of ownership and control has taken place through the multiplication of owners. . . .

Though the American law makes no distinction between the private corporation and the quasi-public, the economics of the two are essentially different. The separation of ownership from control produces a condition where the interests of owner and ultimate manager may, and often do, diverge, and where many of the checks which formerly operated to limit the use of power disappear. Size alone tends to give these giant corporations a social significance not attached to the smaller units of private enterprise. By the use of the open market for securities, each of these corporations assumes obligations towards the investing public which transform it from a legal method clothing the rule of a few individuals into an institution at least nominally serving investors who have embarked their funds in its enterprise. New responsibilities towards owners, the workers, the consumers, and the State thus rest upon the shoulders of those in control. In creating these new relationships, the quasi-public corporation may fairly be said to work a revolution. It has destroyed the unity that we commonly call property — has divided ownership into nominal ownership and the power formerly joined to it. Thereby the corporation has changed the nature of the profit-seeking enterprise. This revolution forms the subject of the present study. . . .

The dissolution of the atom of property destroys the very foundation on which the economic order of the past three hundred years has rested. Private enterprise, which has molded economic life since the close of the middle ages, has been rooted in the institution of private property. . . . Whereas the organization of feudal economic life rested upon an elaborate system of binding customs, the organization under the system of private enterprise has rested upon the self-interest of the property owner — a self-interest held in check only by competition and the conditions of supply and demand. Such self-interest has long been regarded as the best guarantee of economic efficiency. It has been assumed that, if the individual is protected in the right both to use his own property as he sees fit and to receive the full fruits of its use, his desire for personal gain, for profits, can be relied upon as an effective incentive to his efficient use of any industrial property he may possess.

In the quasi-public corporation, such an assumption no longer holds. As we have seen, it is no longer the individual himself who uses his wealth. Those in control of that wealth, and therefore in a position to secure industrial efficiency and product profits, are no longer, as owners, entitled to the bulk of such profits. Those who control the destinies of the typical modern corporation own so insignificant a fraction of the company's stock that the returns from running the corporation profitably accrue to them in only a very minor degree. The stockholders, on the other hand, to whom the profits of the corporation go, cannot be motivated by those profits to a

more efficient use of the property, since they have surrendered all disposition of it to those in control of the enterprise.
The explosion of the atom of property destroys the basis of
the old assumption that the quest for profits will spur the owner
of industrial property to its effective use. It consequently chal-
lenges the fundamental economic principle of individual
initiative in industrial enterprise. It raises for reexamination
the question of the motive force back of industry, and the
ends for which the modern corporation can be or will be run.

The problem of the so-called Berle-Means corporation —that
is, a corporation with centralized management and dispersed
shareholders— is another centerpiece of corporate law and corporate finance in the United States. Indeed, the tension between
the value of retaining managerial discretion (to promote efficiencies in the corporate form, as outlined in Coase's *Nature of the Firm*)
and the dangers of unchecked managerial discretion (as outlined
in the Berle-Means excerpt) is *the* central issue in corporate law.
Much of the Corporations course at law school is devoted to understanding mechanisms of managerial control that protect
investors without unduly constraining the business judgment of
managers. Maintaining this balance in a sensible manner is an
important role of corporate counsel.

As a matter of intellectual history, the interesting point is to
recognize when the problem of managerial discretion in the public corporation was first identified: 1932, in the depths of the Great
Depression and on the eve of the New Deal. Large corporations
with widely dispersed shareholders gained prominence in the
United States only after the First World War. Previously, the major industrial firms tended to be owned by a small number of
extremely wealthy families (such as the Carnegies, Rockefellers,
and Mellons). Only with the boom of the stock market in the 1920s
and the emergence of a large body of retail investors did dispersed
public ownership of corporations become common. So what Professors Berle and Means articulated in their famous book was a
relatively new phenomenon. The acuity of their analysis was,

however, quickly recognized, and it generated support for a number of President Roosevelt's legislative proposals, most notably the principal federal securities laws — the Securities Act of 1933 and the Securities Exchange Act of 1934 — which attempt to tilt the balance of power away from managers and back toward shareholders.

Corporate lawyers in the United States are all intimately familiar with the problem of the Berle-Means corporation. And a host of common corporate activities — from tender offers to proxy fights — are understood as important mechanisms for controlling managerial discretion. (Tender offers and proxy fights are mechanisms that shareholders can use to seize control from managers.) As you will see when you study corporate law, there remains an active debate as to whether these and other mechanisms of control adequately police potential managerial abuses or whether other legal developments (such as poison pills and other takeover defenses) have tipped the balance back in management's favor. We leave the details of these interesting and important issues to another day. For current purposes, what you should recognize is that what Berle and Means identified in their book was a form of the principal-agent problem inherent in the corporate structure. Many of the legal developments that have occurred since their book was written are attempts to resolve this conflict. Analytically, they are similar to the solutions we discussed in the Contracting chapter of *Analytical Methods for Lawyers*: legal requirements designed to make the agent (in this context, the manager) behave in a way that is consistent with the interest of the principal (here, the shareholder).[6]

6. Although the Berle-Means corporation has become a shorthand for conflicts between shareholders and managers of public corporations, the excerpt above (as well as the full book) was also concerned about the expanding power of managers over other parties, particularly workers. And Professors Berle and Means favored public interventions to protect these other parties, sometimes even at the expense of shareholder interests. Modern invocations of the Berle-Means thesis do not usually pick up this strain of the original argument, at least not in the United States.

B. The Roots of Modern Finance

Most academic writing in modern finance is much too technical for an introductory treatment. To give students a sense of the general tenor of this literature, we have provided in this section short excerpts from two seminal works, both of which you are likely to encounter again in upper-level law school courses.

The first is from the initial article of a two-part series in which Professors Modigliani and Miller explored a question that has fascinated financial theorists for many years: how should a firm finance its operations in order to maximize the firm's value? Should firms borrow money (i.e., take out loans) or raise equity (i.e., sell stock)? Or do some combination of the two? Which approach gives the firm the best financing (or the lowest *cost of capital*)? After making a series of simplifying assumptions, the professors reached a startling conclusion: the capital structure of a firm (that is, the proportion of its financing that comes from debt or equity) has *no* impact on its overall value.

Franco Modigliani and Merton H. Miller
The Cost of Capital, Corporation Finance,
and the Theory of Investment
3 *Am. Econ. Rev.* 261, 261–71 (1958)

What is the "cost of capital" to a firm in a world in which funds are used to acquire assets whose yields are uncertain; and in which capital can be obtained by many different media, ranging from pure debt instruments, representing money-fixed claims, to pure equity issues, giving holders only the right to a pro-rata share in the uncertain venture? . . .

In much of his formal analysis, the economic theorist at least has tended to side-step the essence of the cost-of-capital problem by proceeding as though physical assets [e.g., plants and equipment] could be regarded as yielding known, sure streams. Given this assumption, the theorist has concluded that the cost of capital to the owners of a firm is simply the rate of interest on bonds; and has derived the familiar proposition that the firm, acting rationally, will tend to push investment to the point where marginal yield on physical assets is equal to the market rate of interest. . . .

Considered as a convenient approximation, the model of the firm constructed via this certainty — or certainty-equivalent — approach has admittedly been useful in dealing with some of the grosser aspects of the process of capital accumulation. . . . Yet few would maintain that this approximation is adequate. . . .

. . . [A]n alternative approach, based on market value maximization, can provide the basis for an operational definition of the cost of capital and a workable theory of investment. Under this approach any investment project and its concomitant financing plan must pass only the following test: Will the project, as financed, raise the market value of the firm's shares? If so, it is worth undertaking; if not, its return is less than the marginal cost of capital to the firm. . . .

The potential advantages of the market-value approach have long been appreciated; yet analytical results have been meager. What appears to be keeping this line of development from achieving its promise is largely the lack of an adequate theory of the effect of financial structure on market valuations, and of how the effects can be inferred from objective market data. It is with the development of such a theory and of its implications for the cost-of-capital problem that we shall be concerned in this paper.

Our procedure will be to develop . . . the basic theory itself and give some brief account of its empirical relevance. [Then], we show how the theory can be used to answer the cost-of-capital question and how it permits us to develop a theory of investment of the firm under conditions of uncertainty. . . .

[After making a number of simplifying assumptions regarding, among other things, perfect information, frictionless contracting, and the absence of taxation, the paper then begins its formal analysis of the relationship between a firm's financial structure and its market value, and proceeds to defend the following two provocative and influential propositions:]

> Proposition I: . . . *[T]he market value of any firm is independent of its capital structure and is given by capitalizing its expected [stream of profits from its physical assets] at the rate . . . appropriate to the its class. . . . That is, the average cost of capital to any firm is completely independent of its capital structure. . . .*
>
> Proposition II: *[T]he expected yield of a share of stock is equal to the appropriate capitalization rate . . . for a pure equity stream in the class, plus a premium related to the financial risk [associated with the firm's] debt-to-equity ratio.*

At first reading, the language of this excerpt may seem a bit dense, but the essence of the Modigliani and Miller propostions can be easily summarized. In brief, their insight is that the more a firm relies on debt to finance its activities, the more risky and less valuable its equity will become. In the past, financial analysts had assumed that because the interest rate paid on debt is usually cheaper than the cost of a firm's equity, a firm could lower its average cost of capital by financing its activities with more debt and less equity. Modigliani and Miller challenge this once-conventional wisdom by pointing out that the issuance of debt reduces the value of a firm's remaining equity by increasing its riskiness. Through technical analysis that goes beyond the scope of this precis, Modigliani and Miller's article demonstrates that however much a firm saves by issuing new debt, that savings are exactly offset by the reduction in the value of its equity. Thus, a firm's capital structure cannot, in theory, affect a firm's overall value.

What you should also recognize at the outset is that even the authors never believed the propositions summarized above were an accurate reflection of the real world. Rather the propositions were important because they forced financial analysts and academic theorists to think more carefully and systematically about why the choice of capital structures does, in the real word, seem to have an effect on the value of firms. In brief, what subsequent writers (including Modigliani and Miller themselves) have argued is that the choice of capital structure makes a difference in firm value because a number of the simplifying assumptions in the original article are not true in reality. In particular, for certain companies, taxes favor borrowing as compared to the issuance of equity. In addition, costs associated with financial distress and bankruptcy will influence a firm's choice of capital structures.

For a practicing attorney, the importance of this debate is the effect that it has on the activities of corporate clients and their financial advisers. Much of what goes on in the everyday world of corporate finance can be understood as efforts to adjust the capital structure of firms in order to enhance their overall value. For example, when a company issues new stock or retires outstanding debt, the firm is altering its capital structure and (ideally) improving the firm's overall value. Under the stylized assumptions of Modigliani and Miller's original article, these sorts of transactions wouldn't make any sense. But in the real world, they are a staple of everyday corporate practice.

Another important dimension of the choice of capital structure is its effect on the principal-agent problem identified in the Berle-Means excerpt presented above: the tendency of managers in public corporations (agents) not to abide by the interests of their shareholders (principals). In the following famous article, Professors Jensen and Meckling explore how changes in capital structure can be used to resolve that conflict.

Michael C. Jensen and William H. Meckling
Theory of the Firm: Managerial Behavior
3 *J. Fin. Econ.* 35, 36–43 (1976)

Many problems associated with the inadequacy of the current theory of the firm can be viewed as special cases of the theory of agency relationships in which there is a growing literature. . . .

We define an agency relationship as a contract under which one or more persons (the principal(s)) engage another person (the agent) to perform some service on their behalf which involves delegating some decision-making authority to the agent. If both parties to the relationship are utility maximizers there is good reason to believe that the agent will not always act in the best interests of the principal. The *principal* can limit divergences from his interest by establishing appropriate incentives for the agent and by incurring monitoring costs designed to limit the aberrant activities of the agent. In addition in some situations it will pay the *agent* to expend resources (bonding costs) to guarantee that he will not take certain actions which would harm the principal or to ensure that the principal will be compensated if he does take such actions. However, it is generally impossible for the principal or the agent at zero cost to ensure that the agent will make optimal decisions from the principal's viewpoint. In most agency relationships the principal and the agent will incur positive monitoring and bonding costs (non-pecuniary as well as pecuniary), and in addition there will be some divergence between the agent's decisions and those decisions which would maximize the welfare of the principal. The dollar equivalent of the reduction in welfare experienced by the principal due to this divergence is also a cost of the agency relationship, and we refer to this latter cost as the "residual loss." We define agency costs as the sum of:

(1) the monitoring expenditures by the principal,

(2) the bonding expenditures by the agent,

(3) the residual loss . . .

Since the relationship between the stockholders and manager of a corporation fit the definition of a pure agency relationship it should be no surprise to discover that the issues associated with the "separation of ownership and control" in the modern diffuse ownership corporation are intimately associated with the general problem of agency. We show below that an explanation of why and how agency costs generated by the corporate form are born[e] leads to a theory of the ownership (or capital) structure of the firm. . . .

In this section we analyze the effect of outside equity on agency costs by comparing the behavior of a manager when he owns 100 percent of the residual claims on a firm to his behavior when he sells off a portion of those claims to outsiders. If a wholly owned firm is managed by the owner, he will make operating decisions which maximize his utility. These decisions will involve not only the benefits he derives from pecuniary returns but also the utility generated by various non-pecuniary aspects of his entrepreneurial activities such as the physical appointments of the office, the attractiveness of the secretarial staff, the level of employee discipline, the kind and amount of charitable contributions, personal relations ("love", "respect", etc.) with employees, a larger than optimal computer to play with, purchase of production inputs from friends, etc. The optimum mix (in the absence of taxes) of the various pecuniary and non-pecuniary benefits is achieved when the marginal utility derived from an additional dollar of expenditure (measured net of any productive effects) is equal for each non-pecuniary item and equal to the marginal utility derived from an additional dollar of after tax purchasing power (wealth).

If the owner-manager sells equity claims on the corporation which are identical to his (i.e., share proportionately in the profits of the firm and have limited liability)[,] agency costs will be generated by the divergence between his interest and those of the outside shareholders, since he will then bear only a fraction of the costs of any non-pecuniary benefits he takes out in maximizing his own utility. If the manager owns only 95 percent of the stock, he will expend resources to the point where the marginal utility derived from a dollar's expenditure of the firm's resources on such items equals the marginal utility of an additional 95 cents in general purchasing power (i.e., *his* share of the wealth reduction) and not one dollar. Such activities, on his part, can be limited (but probably not eliminated) by the expenditure of resources on monitoring activities by the outside stockholders. But as we show below, the owner will bear the entire wealth effects of these expected costs so long as the equity market anticipates these effects. Prospective minority shareholders will realize that the owner-manager's interests will diverge somewhat from theirs, hence the price which they will pay for shares will reflect the monitoring costs and the effect of the divergence between the manager's interest and theirs. Nevertheless, ignoring for the moment the possibility of borrowing against his wealth, the owner will find it desirable to bear these costs as long as the welfare increment he experiences from converting his claims on the firm into general purchasing power is large enough to offset them.

As the owner-manager's fraction of the equity falls, his fractional claim on the outcomes falls and this will tend to encourage him to appropriate larger amounts of the corporate resources in the form of perquisites. This also makes it desirable for the minority shareholders to expend more resources in monitoring his behavior. Thus, the wealth costs to the owner of obtaining additional cash in the equity markets rise as his fractional ownership falls.

We shall continue to characterize the agency conflict between the owner-manager and outside shareholders as deriving from the manager's tendency to appropriate perquisites out of the firm's resources for his own consumption. However, we do not mean to leave the impression that this is the only or even the most important source of conflict. Indeed, it is likely that the most important conflict arises from the fact that as the manager's ownership claim falls, his incentive to devote significant effort to creative activities such as searching out new profitable ventures falls. He may in fact avoid such ventures simply because it requires too much trouble or effort on his part to manage or to learn about new technologies. Avoidance of these personal costs and the anxieties that go with them also represent a source of on the job utility to him and it can result in the value of the firm being substantially lower than it otherwise could be. . . .

The agency costs of debt

In general if the agency costs engendered by the existence of outside owners are positive it will pay the absentee owner (i.e., shareholders) to sell out to an owner-manager who can avoid these costs. This could be accomplished in principle by having the manager become the sole equity holder by repurchasing all of the outside equity claims with funds obtained through the issued of limited liability debt claims and the sum of his own personal wealth. This single owner corporation would not suffer the agency costs associated with outside equity. Therefore there must be some compelling reasons why we find the diffuse-owner corporate firm financed by equity claims so prevalent as an organizational form.

An ingenious entrepreneur eager to expand, has open to him the opportunity to design a whole hierarchy of fixed claims on assets and earnings, with premiums paid for different levels of risk. Why don't we observe large corporations individually owned with a tiny fraction of the capital supplied by the entrepreneur in return for 100 percent of the equity and the rest simply borrowed? We believe there are a number of reasons: (1) incentive effects associated with highly leveraged firms, (2) monitoring costs these incentive effects engender, and (3) bankruptcy costs. Furthermore, all of these costs are simply particular aspects of the agency costs associated with the existence of debt claims on the firm. . . .

A theory of the corporate ownership structure

In the previous sections we discussed the nature of agency costs associated with outside claims on the firm — both debt and equity. Our purpose here is to integrate these concepts into the beginnings of a theory of the corporate ownership structure. We use the term "ownership structure" rather than "capital structure" to highlight the fact that the crucial variables to be determined are not just the relative amounts of debt and equity but also the fraction of the equity held by the manager. . . .

This Jensen and Meckling excerpt combines elements of our three previous readings in this section. Its title invokes Professor Coase's *Nature of the Firm,* and the Jensen and Meckling article represents a continuation of the Coasean project of attempting to define the optimal set of economic relationships to be organized within the structure of a firm. Jensen and Meckling are arguing that the firm is best structured when equity ownership and managerial control are aligned in the same party. Viewed from this perspective, the Jensen and Meckling excerpt also speaks directly to the problem of the Berle-Means corporation: one way to eliminate the problems of unbridled managerial discretion inherent in public corporations is to encourage managers to become (once again) the owners of their own firms — that is, to privatize the public corporation. Finally, Jensen and Meckling are writing in the Modigliani and Miller tradition because, at root, Jensen and Meckling are addressing the optimal capital structure of the firm. In advancing their argument, Jensen and Meckling are balancing the value-enhancing properties of aligning management and ownership against the costs of maintaining high levels of debt.

The Jensen and Meckling thesis also has real-world applications. Since this article was written in 1976, corporate takeovers have become increasingly common. In some of these transactions, a small group of investors backed with large quantities of debt (a.k.a. junk bonds) acquire a public firm. These investor groups are pursuing precisely the strategy that Jensen and Meckling have advocated. By substituting themselves for a large group of public shareholders, these investor groups hope to improve control over corporate management (i.e., restrain unbridled discretion) and thereby enhance corporate value. The debate over the propriety and efficacy of these transactions is fascinating and as yet unresolved, but there is no question that their intellectual foundations can be traced back to Professors Jensen and Meckling and the academic traditions upon which their article is based.

C. The Goals of Finance

The foregoing excerpts suggest some of the critical questions that financial theory seeks to address. How much economic activity should be located within a particular firm? How can we make sure that the managers of firms remain faithful to the interests of their principals (traditionally understood to be their shareholders)? What is the best capital structure for a particular firm? Should it have more or less debt? Should its shares of common stock be distributed broadly to many shareholders, or should they be concentrated in the hands of a small number of individuals who can more easily keep track of the firm's activities?

To answer these questions, financial theorists have developed a number of techniques, several of which are introduced in the balance of this chapter. Many of these techniques provide tools for analysts to estimate the value of business activities (such as the construction of a new plant) that will generate benefits over extended periods of time. Others techniques look to the performance of a firm's stock in the capital markets as a means of measuring the company's riskiness and also the quality of its managers' performance. Armed with these and related tools, the financial analyst can offer guidance as to whether a firm should launch a new product or make an adjustment in its capital structure or even replace existing management with new blood.

In the following section, we summarize several basic financial techniques that are characteristic of the field and also of particular relevance to practicing attorneys. We begin in the next section with one of the most fundamental financial concepts: the time value of money. Then we turn to several more complex but equally important tenets of modern finance.

3. The Time Value of Money

One basic financial principle that all lawyers should understand is the relationship between the value of money today and the value of money in the future. This relationship is sometimes described as the *time value of money*. This section introduces the concept and illustrates its relevance to the practice of law.

A. Comparing Current Dollars to Future Dollars

A choice that attorneys often face is helping clients decide whether to accept a payment immediately or to get a somewhat larger payment at some point in future. Suppose, for example, you were representing a plaintiff with a wrongful discharge claim against his former employer. And suppose further that the employer offered your client a $1,000 payment to settle the dispute but that you were confident that, if litigated, the claim would generate $1,100 for your client (net of attorney's fees and all other expenses). The only fact you didn't know was how long it would take for the suit to be litigated. How can you help your client decide whether to accept the $1,000 settlement offer today or reject the offer and litigate the claim?[7]

One way of approaching this problem would be to calculate how much money your client would have if he accepted the settlement offer, put the funds into a bank account, and kept the funds there until the litigation was completed. Comparing the future balance of such a hypothetical bank account with the expected subsequent court award offers a good initial illustration of the

---

7. Some students who are familiar with decision analysis may recognize that this presentation omits various potential complexities. In most cases there will be uncertainty as to the amount of a litigated award, and so multiple possible awards might have to be analyzed or, perhaps, analysis of an expected award would be more appropriate. In addition, one might want to consider the possibility that the defendant will raise its settlement offer if you choose to proceed to trial. Also, there is a possibility that the award of pre-judgment interest might increase the amount of an award the longer the trial is delayed. We omit these and other complexities here in order to focus on the time-value-of-money issue.

time value of money. To complete the analysis, you need to know (or estimate) the rate of interest your client could earn on a bank deposit. Let's say, after investigation, that interest paid on a bank account turns out to be 5% a year. So, if the settlement payment stayed in the bank account for 1 year, it would grow to $1,050, which is $1,000 plus 5% of $1,000. In mathematical notation, you would typically write this as

$$\$1,000 + 0.05 \times \$1,000 = \$1,000 \, (1 + 0.05)$$
$$= \$1,050$$

(Remember that the term *percent* means *for every one hundred;* thus, 5% is 5 divided by 100, or 0.05.)

So, if you knew the litigation would be over at the end of 1 year, you would know that the litigated value of the case — $1,100 — is a bit greater than the value of putting the settlement offer into a bank account for 1 year — $1,050. But what if the litigation would take 2 years to complete? At this point, one might be tempted to say that since we got $50 of interest on the account in the first year, then we'll get another $50 the second year, giving us exactly $1,100 in the account at the end of 2 years. This simplistic approach is, however, wrong. In year 2, interest is being paid on $1,050 (the original amount plus interest earned during the first year) and not on $1,000 (just the original amount). In other words, the simplistic approach fails to take account of the interest paid in year 2 on interest earned the first year. Properly calculated, by the end of year 2, the balance in the account would be equal to $1,050 plus 5% of $1,050, or $1,102.50:

$$5\% \text{ of } \$1,050 = 0.05 \times \$1,050$$
$$= \$52.50$$

so

$$\$1,050 \times (1.05) = \$1,050 + \$52.50$$
$$= \$1,102.50$$

Thus, your client would be slightly better off accepting the settlement offer and leaving it in a bank account earning 5% interest for 2 years than going to trial and receiving a net settlement of $1,100 at the of 2 years. What's more, the longer the trial took to complete, the more attractive the immediate settlement offer would become. In the language of decision analysis, the crossover point for choosing the immediate settlement offer or going to trial is a bit less than 2 years.

To abstract a bit from the foregoing illustration, one can see the basic structure of the time value of money. After 1 year, the bank account is worth $1,000 \times (1 + 0.05)$. After 2 years, the account is worth $1,050 \times (1 + 0.05)$, which can be rewritten as $1,000 \times (1 + 0.05) \times (1 + 0.05)$. (Do you see why?) Getting a bit more mathematical, this last expression can be written in the following shorthand: $1,000 \times (1 + 0.05)^2$. If the money stayed in the account for 5 years, it would have a value of $1,000 \times (1 + 0.05)^5$, which is $1,276.28. If the money stayed in the account for 10 years, it would have a value of $1,000 \times (1 + 0.05)^{10}$, or $1,628.89. And so on.[8]

B. Simple versus Compound Interest

Let's return a moment to the simplistic, but erroneous, method of calculating interest mentioned in the preceding subsection. Projecting the interest to be paid in future years based on the interest generated in year 1 has a certain appeal. It is easy to do, and for short periods of time, the use of this method (known as simple interest) is not that much different than the more accurate technique described above (known as compound interest). In our example, using interest of $50 per year yielded a value at the end of year 2 of $1,100, only slightly off from the correct value of $1,102.50. Over longer periods, however, the differences can be

---

8. More generally, the future value (FV) of a sum of money (PV) deposited into a bank account yielding a given rate of interest (r) over a specified number of years (n) can be described by this equation: $FV = PV \times (1 + r)^n$.

large, and before too long astronomical. In the example given above, after 10 years the amount in the bank account under compound interest was $1,628.89. That means the accrued interest ($628.89) was $128.89 more than what would have been projected with simple interest ($500.00, or 10 × $50).

The power of compound interest is one of the enduring miracles of finance, and its effect on the time value of money is often much larger than one's intuitions would suggest, particularly with higher interest rates. One heuristic that is worth remembering is the Rule of 72 — which is a rough guide for the number of years it takes a sum of money to double under compound interest. If you divide 72 by the annual rate of interest, the answer is a fairly accurate estimate of the number of years it takes money to increase by 100% — that is, to double. So money deposited into a bank account paying 5% will double in roughly 14.4 years (72/5). You can check this prediction using our example above. If you left your immediate settlement of $1,000 in the bank for 14 years, it would equal $1,000 × (1 + 0.05)^{14}, or $1,979.93, just shy of $2,000. Figure 1 sum-

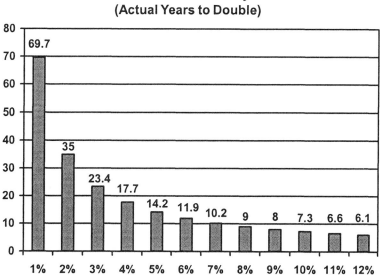

Figure 1
How Fast Does Your Money Grow?
(Actual Years to Double)

marizes the actual doubling period for a sum growing at a compound interest rate for a range of interest rates.

C. Finding the Present Value of a Single Future Payment

Another common problem that arises in many legal contexts is trying to calculate the current value of a payment to be made at some point in the future. For example, suppose a client of yours wins a lottery entitling the client to the payment of $1 million at the end of 1 year. Suppose further that the state lottery commission offers to make a somewhat smaller payment — say $940,000 — but will make that payment immediately. How should you advise your client?

Clearly, this problem is quite similar to the problems we discussed above — choosing between an immediate settlement offer and a somewhat larger expected award after trial. There, we were calculating the future value of a sum received now. Here, we are asking about the present value of a sum to be received in the future. The way lawyers (and financial analysts) solve these two sorts of problems is also quite similar. If we can figure out what sum of money placed in a bank account with the appropriate interest rate would grow to $1 million at the end of a year, then we would know the present value of that $1 million lottery payment. Restated more formally — and assuming that 5% is still the right rate of interest — we are trying to calculate a sum of money that, if multiplied by (1 + 0.05), equals 1,000,000:

$$\text{present value} \times (1 + 0.05) = \$1 \text{ million}$$

And, dividing both sides of the equation by (1 + 0.05), you find

$$\text{present value} = \$1 \text{ million}/(1 + 0.05)$$
$$= \$952,380.95$$

So the lottery commission's offer of $940,000 is a bit lower than the present value of $1 million in a year's time. While there may be other reasons for your client to take the money right now —

who wants to wait a year to be a millionaire? — our financial analysis would counsel otherwise.

With this basic approach, one can evaluate the present value of payments to be made much further in the future. Suppose the lottery commission were not required to make its $1 million payment until 4 years had passed. What would the present value be under those circumstances? Intuitively, you may sense that the further in the future the payment is, the lower the present value must be, and that's exactly right. Again, a helpful way to frame the problem is to consider how much money you would have to put in the bank today in order to have $1 million in 4 years. Following the analysis presented above:

present value $\times (1 + 0.05) \times (1 + 0.05) \times (1 + 0.05) \times (1 + 0.05) = \$1$ million

And, dividing both sides of the equation by $(1 + 0.05)^4$, you find

$$\text{present value} = \$1 \text{ million}/(1 + 0.05)^4$$
$$= \$822,702.47$$

Just as the power of compound interest increases the size of a bank account over time, similar factors enhance the discount of payments that will not be made until far in the future.[9]

D. Valuing a Stream of Future Payments

A variant on the foregoing problem involves the calculation of the present value of a series (or stream) of future payments. Lawyers face this problem when they receive settlement offers in the form of a proposal to make 10 payments of $50,000 annually for 10 years. Such a settlement might be plausible in a tort case where a 55-year-old plaintiff had been incapacitated in such a way that it was no longer possible for the plaintiff to work. A series of

---

9. The general formula for the present value (PV) of a payment to be received a specified number of years (n) in the future (FV) is $PV = FV/(1 + r)^n$, where r is the appropriate interest rate. Notice that this equation is simply a restatement of the formula given in the previous footnote, after dividing both sides by $(1 + r)^n$.

$50,000 payments could be viewed as replacing wages for the rest
of the plaintiff's working life. The question a lawyer would have
to consider is whether it would be better to accept this structured
settlement or a lump-sum settlement of, say, $400,000.

In practice, most lawyers (and even most financial analysts)
would use a calculator or computer program to answer questions
of this sort. But we have already developed sufficient analytical
tools to figure out the answer ourselves. You can simply break up
the settlement proposal into 10 separate payments of $50,000. (See
Figure 2, Option A.) You already know how to figure out the
present value of the first payment, which is received at the end of
the first year. As long as the 5% interest rate is still appropriate,
the present value is $50,000/(1 + 0.05), or $47,619.05. (Note: this
is the same calculation we did above for the $1 million lottery
payment at the end of a year.) And you can make a similar calculation for the 9 other payments:

$$\text{present value} = \$50,000/(1 + .05) +$$
$$\$50,000/(1 + .05)^2 +$$
$$\$50,000/(1 + .05)^3 +$$
$$\cdots$$
$$\$50,000/(1 + .05)^{10}$$

$$= \$47,619 +$$
$$\$45,351 +$$
$$\$43,192 +$$
$$\cdots$$
$$\$30,696$$

$$= \$386,087$$

So $400,000 looks pretty good by comparison. (Another way of
thinking about this analysis is to recognize that if you put $400,000
into a bank account yielding 5% interest and took out $50,000 a
year for 10 years, there would be something left in the account at
the end of 10 years.)

Figure 2
Periodic Payments v. Lump Sum Payment
Option A:
Ten Payments of $50,000 each Over Ten Years

$50,000 $50,000 $50,000   · · · · $50,000

Year One   Year Two   Year Three   Year Ten

Option B:
One Payment of $400,000 Today

$400,000

· · · ·

Today   Year One   Year Two   Year Three   Year Ten

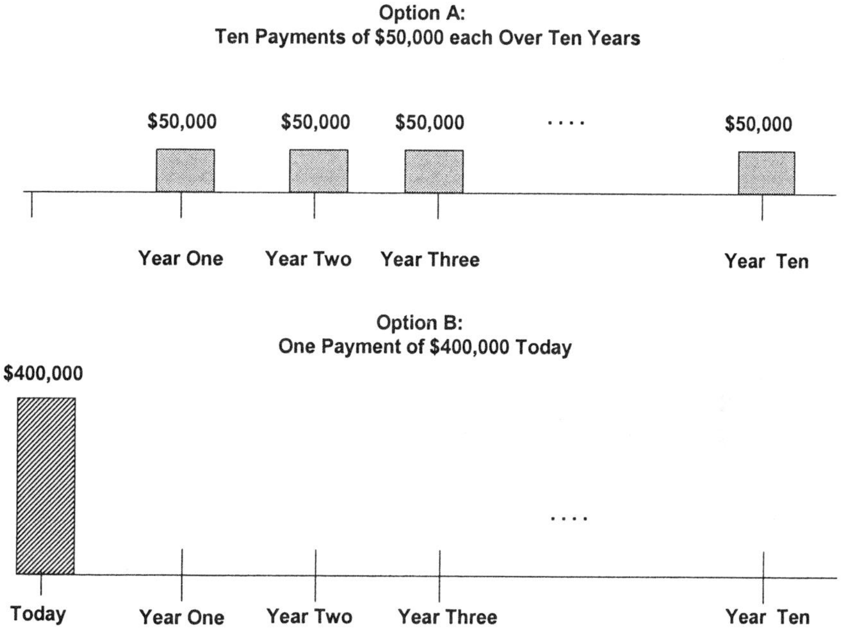

Streams of payments are surprisingly common in legal settings. Oftentimes, the payments will be made for the remainder of a person's life. In that context, the payment is known as an annuity, and many retirement benefits as well as some tort settlements are made in this manner. In order to value payment streams of this sort, one must estimate life expectancies as well as appropriate interest rates. Financial textbooks devote considerable attention to the valuation of annuities and derive a number of helpful formulas for calculating their present value.[10]

---

10. For example, the present value (PV) of a perpetual (i.e., continuing forever) annual annuity (P) discounted at an interest rate (r) has a quite simple formula: $PV = P/r$. The present value (PV) of a perpetual annuity that grows at a given annual rate (g) has this formula: $PV = P/(r - g)$. If you're interested in reviewing the derivation of these and similar formulas, you should consult Ross, et al., *Corporate Finance* (2003).

Box 1
Present Value or Future Value

When comparing present payments and future payments, you can either convert the present values into future values (as we did in section A) or convert future values into present values (as we did in section C). Both approaches work. The key is to express the payments to be compared in the values associated with the same time period. You want to compare apples with apples and oranges with oranges.

In practice, analysts almost always use the latter technique: converting future values into present values. There are a number of reasons for this convention. Most notably, most people find it easier to understand payments expressed in terms of present values. The dollars in your wallet right now are "present value" dollars. If we determine that a future payment has a present value of $100, what we mean is that the future payment has the same value as $100 in your wallet.

E. Internal Rates of Return

So far in this section, we have been trying to figure the present or future value of cash payments. To make these valuations, we have had to make certain assumptions about the appropriate interest rate to use. And, for simplicity's sake, we have been using a 5% rate of interest. Sometimes, however, financial problems arise the other way around: we know the present and future values of a transaction, and what we need to figure out is the interest rate implicit in the cash stream. In financial argot, this is called the *internal rate of return.* Suppose you have a 55 year-old client who wants to deposit $30,000 in a bank account to use for the client's retirement that will begin in ten years. Suppose further the bank offers your the following two choices: either the deposit can earn 10 percent per year on the deposit, compounded annually, over the ten year period or your client can receive a single payment of $100,000 at the end of the ten year period. Which option should you choose?

You could approach this problem in several ways. One approach would be to calculate the value of the bank account after ten years, growing at a compounded interest rate of 10 percent per year. From our prior discussions, we know how to do this calculation of future values:

$$\text{Future Value} = \text{initial deposit} \times (1 + \text{annual interest rate})^{(\text{number of years})}$$
$$= \$30{,}000 \times (1 + 0.10)^{10}$$
$$= \$30{,}000 \times (2.59)$$
$$= \$77{,}812$$

Based on this analysis, you can tell that it's better for your client to take the second choice, which promises a $100,000 payment at the end of ten years (in contrast to the $77,812 payment implicit in a 10 percent rate of interest on a bank deposit).

But what if you wanted to know exactly how high the bank's stated rate of interest on a ten-year deposit would have to be in order to offer your client a better return than the second option? This might be a relevant question if you were shopping around at other banks that offered a range of different interest rates.

One somewhat clunky method is trial and error, whereby you would experiment with a number of possible interest rates and see which one does the best job of making $30,000 grow into $100,000 at the end of 10 years. We already know that a 10% interest rate is too low (it generates only $77,812 after 10 years). So 10% is too low, how about 15%?

$$\$30{,}000 \times (1 + 0.15)^{10} = \$30{,}000 \times 4.046$$
$$= \$121{,}366.70$$

That's closer to the mark ($100,000) but a bit too high. Perhaps something on the order of 12% would be more appropriate:

$$\$30{,}000 \times (1 + 0.12)^{10} = \$30{,}000 \times 3.106$$
$$= \$93{,}175.40$$

Better, but still not quite right. But you can see how we might proceed with this methodology.

Another approach is to resort to a financial calculator, which will perform essentially the same iterative operations (but much more quickly) and then tell you that the exact interest rate needed to grow $30,000 into $100,000 at the end of ten years is 12.7945%. In other words,

$$\$30,000 \times (1 + 0.127945)^{10} = \$30,000 \times 3.33$$
$$= \$100,000$$

What this calculation suggests is that the second option presented to your client — a promise of $100,000 at the end of ten years on an initial deposit of $30,000 — carries an implicit interest rate of 12.79% per year compounded annually. With this analysis you could advise your client that it would make sense to choose the bank's second option unless another bank were offering to pay an interest rate of more than 12.79% on a 10-year deposit. Internal rates of return are also used in various other legal and financial contexts, such as the evaluation of investment opportunities.

F. What Interest Rate Should You Use?

So far in our discussion, we've skipped over one of the most difficult and important aspects of time-value-of-money techniques: selecting an appropriate interest rate. Because of the properties of compound interest, changes in interest rate assumptions can make a huge difference in valuations. Just looking back to the preceding section, we saw that $30,000 invested at 10% grows to less than $78,000 at the end of 10 years, but at 12.79% grows to a full $100,000. Particularly when dealing with longer periods of time, present and future value calculations are highly sensitive to interest rate assumptions.

In practice, the role of selecting the correct interest rate assumptions will usually fall to financial professionals. Investment bankers typically do this sort of analysis in major transactions, and oftentimes clients will have considerable in-house expertise in the area. Even in these contexts, however, attorneys should have a general idea of what is going on. Moreover, for smaller corporate clients and individual clients, the lawyer will often be the most financially sophisticated participant in a transaction. In these contexts, the lawyer's advice may be crucial. In the land of the blind, the one-eyed man (or woman) is king (or queen).

Crudely speaking, there are three different ways to think about selecting an interest rate. The second has the greatest analytical purity — and is the one most analogous to the approach that financial analysts typically follow — but the first and the third offer practical guidance that may have considerable salience in certain contexts.

1. Current return on your own savings. In the initial illustrations discussed in this section of the chapter, we made reference to the rate of interest paid by your client's bank. In some contexts, this may be a wholly sensible way of proceeding. For a tort victim who is going to use a settlement payment to pay future expenses — cover lost wages and costs associated with rehabilitation — there is a certain appeal to using an interest rate that describes what the client will earn on the funds. There are, however, certain problems with this approach. For one thing, this approach implicitly equates funds deposited in a bank with payments due from other parties who may well be substantially less creditworthy than a regulated financial institution and almost certainly not covered by federal deposit insurance. Depending on the context, this difference may have more or less significance. If the future payment is to come in a year or two and the payer is General Motors, then maybe the difference in risk is not that important. On the other hand, if the future payment is not due for 5 years and is coming from a start-up enterprise that may well go bankrupt in the meantime, then the risk differential would be highly relevant, and using a bank interest rate to discount future payments would be problematic in that it would overvalue future payments.

2. A rate based on the characteristics of the payer. A second, alternative approach is to peg interest rates to the risk characteristics of the entity or individual who is going to be making the payment. With this approach, the interest rate used to value future payment would be relatively low if the payment were to come from the federal government (which is generally thought to be the payer least likely to default on its obligation), somewhat higher for General Motors, and higher still for high-technology companies and most individual payers. While the intuitive appeal of this risk-adjusted approach is clear, exactly how you should go about determining the precise interest rates to use for different payers is not. Indeed, a large proportion of financial theory deals with adjusting rates of return to account for the varying degrees of risk of different payers. Later on in this chapter — when we introduce the so-called Capital Asset Pricing Model — we will explore the most common technique for estimating the riskiness of firms with publicly traded common stock. And, if you were helping a client to select an interest rate for discounting future promises of some firms, you would likely employ the Capital Asset Pricing Model and similarly spirited techniques.

Crudely speaking, what these financial techniques attempt to do is estimate how much particular firms have to pay to raise funds in the capital market. Once you know what the market is charging a firm for funds, that information gives you a benchmark for determining how much your client should discount future payments from the firm. So, let's go back. Imagine, for example, you had a client who was offered a $100,000 payment in ten years as settlement for a contract dispute. But, suppose this offer is not coming from a bank, but rather from a building contractor. Based on calculations we did in the preceding section, we know the present value of $100,000 in ten years discounted at 12.79% is $30,000. (Do you remember why?) But what if we knew that other creditors were charging the building contractor interest rates of 20% to borrow money? That would suggest that a promise from the contractor to pay $100,000 in ten years has less than a $30,0000 present value. Indeed, $100,000 discounted at a 20% interest rate over ten years has a present value of only $16,151.

As the foregoing illustration suggests, moving from an interest rate based on the rate of return on your client's savings account to a rate of return based on the payer's cost of borrowing can have a profound effect on your present value calculations. With an interest rate of 5%, the present value of $100,000 at the end of 10 years is $61,391.33 ($100,000 divided by $[1 + 0.05]^{10}$), which is more than twice as much as the value of $30,000 that was based on a 12.79% interest rate. Similarly, raising the discount rate to 20% reduces the present value of $100,000 in ten years by nearly half again, to only $16,151.

3. Your own costs of borrowing funds. While conceptually attractive, it may not always be practical or even appropriate to use the payer's cost of funds to calculate present values. Imagine, for example, that your client's delicatessen had been destroyed as a result of flooding from a broken water main. To get the store open again, your client needs to spend $50,000 immediately. Your client's only way to get the money right now is to run up her personal credit cards, which charge an annual interest rate of 20%. The water company, which has an AAA (i.e., very good) credit rating, offers you the choice of either $48,000 right now or $56,000 at the end of a year. Which offer should your client accept? Well, if you employed a discount rate based on the water company's credit rating, you would probably opt for the later payment. A payment of $56,000 is 16.67% greater than $48,000 ($56,000 is $8,000 more than $48,000, and $8,000 is 16.67% of $48,000). So, as long as the water company's cost of borrowing was less than 16.67%, the present value of $56,000 discounted at the payer's cost of borrowing will be greater than $48,000. Your client, however, would be worse off taking the later payment, because your client is forced to borrow at 20% on high-cost credit cards. Another way of making this point is to note that, discounted at your client's cost of borrowing (20%), $56,000 has a net present value of $46,666.67 ($56,000 divided by [1 + 0.20]), which is less than the immediate settlement offer of $48,000.[11]

4. Risk aversion, again. Before leaving the issue of selecting interest rates, we should note that issues of risk aversion also arise in this context. Just because you have adjusted a future payment into a present value does not mean that you have addressed the issue of risk aversion. You still need to consider whether the various outcomes being evaluated might have an especially bad consequence for your client — for example, small future payouts in some situations where your clients will have large needs.

In addition, when employing interest rates based on the payer's cost of borrowing derived from market-based prices, one must be aware that the market has a unique way of evaluating risks. We will deal with this issue in more detail in the next section of this chapter, but the important point to recognize is that the market tends not to factor in risks that can be eliminated through diversification, but rather includes only nondiversifiable risks. In many legal contexts, your clients will not have a diversified portfolio of claims against a sufficiently large group of payers. So in these contexts, unconsidered reliance on a market-derived cost of funds may be inappropriate.

---

11. Figuring out when it is appropriate to use the payer's cost of funds as opposed to the recipient's opportunity costs can be tricky. As mentioned above, financial analysts prefer to use a payer's-cost-of-funds approach. This will be appropriate in situations in which the recipient can sell the payer's obligation into some sort of market. So, in the case described above, if your client could sell the water company's commitment to make a $56,000 payment at the end of the year, the market would presumably value the claim based on the water company's cost of funds, and then that rate would be the appropriate discount rate for your client. In practice, however, not all future claims can be liquidated in this manner. Accordingly, in some contexts, relying upon your client's cost of borrowing will be appropriate.

G. Take-Home Lessons on the Time Value of Money

Although it takes some time and practice to get comfortable with the time value of money, the rudiments of this analytical method are fairly straightforward. As a general rule, money in the future is worth less than the same amount of money today. Exactly how much less depends on both how far in the future the future payment is to be made and which interest rate you use to discount the future payment. The further in the future, the lower the present value, and the higher the discount rate, the lower the present value. If you keep these basic principles in mind, you are well on the way to understanding the time value of money.

4. Key Concepts in Corporate Finance

We turn now from the time value of money, which is an analytical tool with a broad range of applications, to a more specialized set of concepts developed for use in the field of corporate finance. Our discussion will cover four fundamental and related topics: efficient market hypotheses, the relationship between risk and return; the benefits of diversification; and the capital asset pricing model.

A. The Efficient Market Hypotheses

Oftentimes, both in law school classrooms and in legal practice, reference will be made to the *efficiency* of the stock market. When used in this context, efficiency means more than operating in a cost-effective manner. It implies something about the prices of securities traded on the markets. In casual usage, people sometimes equate stock market efficiency with the fundamental correctness of stock market prices. For example, you might hear someone say, "I know IBM stock is really worth $150 a share because that's what it's trading at on the stock market and the market is efficient." Formally speaking, however, market efficiency has a narrower meaning or, more accurately, a narrower set of meanings. The following excerpt from a well-known law review article explains.

Ronald J. Gilson and Reinier H. Kraakman
The Mechanisms of Market Efficiency
70 *Va. L. Rev.* 549 (1984)

Of all recent developments in financial economics, the efficient capital market hypothesis ("ECMH") has achieved the widest acceptance by the legal culture. It now commonly informs the academic literature on a variety of topics; it is addressed by major law school casebooks and textbooks on business law; it structures debate over the future of securities regulation both within and without the Securities and Exchange Commission; it has served as the intellectual premise for a major revision of the disclosure system administered by the Commission; and it has even begun to influence judicial decisions and the actual practice of law. In short, the ECMH is now the context in which serious discussion of the regulation of financial markets takes place. . . .

The fixation on the fact of market efficiency has also characterized much of the financial economics literature on the ECMH. Professor Jensen has stated that "there is no other proposition in economics which has more empirical evidence supporting it than the efficient market hypothesis." Despite certain anomalies, numerous studies demonstrate that the capital market responds efficiently to an extraordinary variety of information. Indeed in the single area of financial accounting data, even the number of surveys of empirical studies of capital market efficiency is substantial. . . .[12]

The language of efficient capital market theory reveals its origins as a vocabulary of empirical description. The common definition of market efficiency, that "prices at any time 'fully reflect' all available information," is really a shorthand for the empirical claim that "available information" does not

---

12. See, e.g., . . . P. Griffin, *Usefulness to Investors and Creditors of Information Provided by Financial Reporting: A Review of Empirical Accounting Research* (1981). . . .

support profitable trading strategies or arbitrage opportunities. Similarly, Eugene Fama's landmark 1970 review article first proposed the now-familiar division of the ECMH into "weak," "semi-strong," and "strong" forms as a device for classifying empirical tests of price behavior.[24]

- Weak tests examined the claim that the histories of securities prices could not yield lucrative trading opportunities.[25]
- Semi-strong form tests probed the same prediction about categories of publicly available information of obvious information to investors.[26]
- Finally, strong form tests examined the extension of the hypothesis to information that was available only to particular groups of privileged investors [e.g., cor-

---

24. [Eugene Fama, Efficient Capital Markets: A Review of Theory and Empirical Work, 25 *J. Fin.* 383, 388 (1970)]. Fama credited Harry Roberts with distinguishing weak and strong form tests. Id. at 383 n.1.

25. Id. at 389–96 (review of tests). Numerous weak form tests support the hypothesis that the history of securities prices does not yield exploitable trading opportunities. . . . Generally, these tests take two forms: serial correlation analyses, which establish little or no relationship between changes in securities prices over successive periods. . . .; and analyses of "filter rule" trading strategies, which reject the possibility that trading on complex patterns of price movements of the sort employed by "chartists" can yield abnormal returns.

26. [Id.] at 404–09 (reviewing empirical tests). Studies of semi-strong form efficiency are tests of how long market prices require to adjust to price-relevant information that is released to the public. These studies typically ask whether trading activity that follows the release of such information can earn investors abnormally high returns and focus on the security's price history before and after the trading period. . . . The discovery of abnormal returns indicates trading opportunities and, therefore, possible market inefficiency. The results thus far indicate efficient price responses to a wide variety of publicly released information, ranging from earning reports and dividend announcements to accounting changes, stock splits, press evaluations, and even changes in Federal Reserve policy. . . . Not all semi-strong form tests indicate market efficiency, however.

porate insiders].[27]

In this usage, the weak, semi-strong, and strong form categories have proved both useful and precise. The hypothesized dearth of arbitrage opportunities, whatever its explanation, clearly grows in strength with each successive genre of test. The more private the information, the more intuitively reasonable the proposition that one might profit by trading on it, and so the stronger the opposing claim that such profitable trading is impossible.

Over time, however, scholars have pressed the weak, semi-strong, and strong form categories beyond their original service as a classification of empirical tests into more general duty as a classification of market responses to particular kinds of information. For example, prices might be said to incorporate efficiently one genre of information that is semi-strong or public, but fail to reflect another that is strong form, or non-public. Indeed, taken a step further, scholars sometimes describe markets themselves as weak, semi-strong, or strong form efficient. Without ever being quite explicit, this powerful shorthand implies that different market dynamics are involved in the reflection of different kinds of information into price, and that varying degrees of market efficiency might well be the consequence.

27. [Id.] at 409–13 (reviewing strong form tests). Unlike weak and semi-strong form tests, which probe trading opportunities that might arise from particular kinds of information . . . strong form studies cannot test for analogous opportunities arising from the generation of non-public information because investigators are unlikely to learn about such information (or if they do, they are unlikely to employ it for research purposes). For this reason, strong form tests must probe indirectly for trading opportunities arising from non-public information. Such tests seek to identify investors who are likely to possess non-public information and to determine whether these traders consistently earn net returns higher than the market average. The results have been mixed. Corporate insiders, such as officers, directors and affiliated bankers, systematically outperform the market. So do specialists on the major stock exchanges who posses non-public information about unexecuted orders. . . . Mutual funds, however, appear to outperform the market only enough to cover administrative and trading costs.

As the Gilson and Kraakman excerpt indicates, the various permutations of the efficient market hypothesis all deal with *informational* efficiency. Technically speaking, the hypotheses simply predict that investors cannot use certain kinds of information (whether past price movements in the weak form, public information in the semi-strong form, or private information in the strong form) to achieve better-than-average profits from stock market investments. The hypotheses postulate that market prices already take these categories of information into account. Importantly, the efficient market hypotheses do not speak directly to the fundamental correctness of stock market prices. For example, many internet companies with high stock market valuations in the late 1990s ended up in bankruptcy a few years later, and — in retrospect — their previous valuations turned out to be wrong. These outcomes, however, do not undermine the efficient market hypotheses because the hypotheses do not concern long term or ultimate values. Moreover, the fact that the value of the entire stock market declined dramatically in 2000 through 2002 does not refute the efficient market hypotheses unless the decline could have been predicted based on one of the sets of information that market prices were to have impounded.[12]

12. Most of the empirical evidence supporting the efficient market hypothesis is drawn from studies of large U.S. markets, principally the New York Stock Exchange and the NASDAQ market, where large quantities of securities are traded and many analysts are following each class of security. In markets where there is less trading or where prices are determined in different ways, informational efficiency may not be present. In the extreme, imagine that a company offered to sell you some stock for $100 a share in a private transaction to which you and the company were the only parties. The market would have no role in setting the price of that stock, and so there would be no reason to believe the $100 proposed price was, in any meaningful sense, efficient. Accordingly, one needs to be careful not to extend the lessons of the ECMH literature to other kinds of markets when its applicability has not been demonstrated.

Box 2

Market Efficiency and Behavioral Finance

Even before the marked decline in the US stock market in the past few years, some financial theorists were reconsidering the validity of prior claims about stock market efficiency. In part, this reconsideration was based on additional empirical studies suggesting a variety of "anomalies" in stock market performance that appeared to contradict the efficient market hypothesis. For example, one set of studies suggested that investors might be able to use certain kinds of historical information (like the ratio of a company's market value to its book value) to predict the future performance of common stock. Other theorists speculated that irrational exuberance and other psychological factors may cause financial and other markets to suffer from fads and trends, in the extreme culminating in bubbles, during which prices rise to what subsequently appear to be unreasonable levels. Think tulip bulbs in the first half of the 17th century. While market efficiency remains an important landmark of financial theory, the scope of its domain is likely to remain contested for some time. For a sympathetic and informative introduction to this critique of market efficiency, see Andrei Shleifer, *Inefficient Markets: An Introduction to Behavioral Finance* (2000).

The efficient capital market hypotheses have had an extraordinary influence on legal developments over the past few decades. Their impact is most pronounced, naturally enough, in the field of securities regulation. Consider, for example, the plaintiff's burden of proof in a securities fraud case. Traditionally, to prove fraud a plaintiff would have to introduce evidence that the plaintiff relied on a defendant's fraudulent statement, typically by showing that the plaintiff had heard or read the fraudulent statement and then purchased the defendant's securities as a result of that information. In light of the ECMH, courts for the past twenty years have generally waived this traditional showing of reliance for shares of stock purchased in stock market transactions on the ground that the stock market price of the securities would have impounded the defendant's fraudulent statement and so when a plaintiff purchases securities at the market price the plaintiff indirectly relied on the defendant's fraudulent statement. This innovation in legal doctrine — known as the fraud-on-the-market theory — has greatly facilitated the prosecution of securities claims and is a direct result of the ECMH.

The efficient capital market hypothesis has also been influential in other legal settings. Consider, for example, compensation arrangements for corporate managers. In the Accounting chapter, we talked a bit about how compensation might be tied to various accounting measures, such as return on assets or return on equity. As we saw, however, financial statements are an imperfect reflection of economic reality. If a company developed an extremely valuable new patent, its economic value might increase substantially, but there would be no accounting impact (because of the accounting treatment of intangible assets). So, if the chief executive officer's compensation were based on an accounting measure of profitability, the impact of the new patent would not be reflected. If, on the other hand, compensation were tied to the performance of the company's stock, then (as a result of the market's informational efficiency) the impact of the new patent would be taken into account.[13] For this and other reasons, managerial compensation of top executives in public companies is increasingly tied to stock market performance.

---

13. If the relevant market were efficient in only the semi-strong sense, news of the patent would need to be disclosed to the public for the information to be reflected in the company's stock price. If the market were strong-form efficient — a more debatable proposition — then the discovery would be impounded into stock prices even without public disclosure.

B. Risk and Return

A second fundamental financial concept of importance to law-yers is the trade-off between risk and return. In finance, "risk" and "return" are terms of art and warrant careful consideration.

The return on a financial asset is the total economic benefit that an asset generates over a certain period of time, typically a year. Economic benefit can come in the form of periodic payments, such as interest in bonds or dividends on stock, or in the form of ap-preciation in value. So, if a share of common stock increased in value from $100 dollars at the beginning of the year to $110 at the end of the year, the value of the stock would have appreci-ated 10% ($10 appreciation divided by $100 beginning price per share) over the course of the year. If the common stock also paid a $5 dividend at the end of the year, its total annual return would be 15% ($10 appreciation plus $5 dividend divided by $100 be-ginning price per share).

Risk, in contrast, is a measure of expected variation in return. In other words, risk relates to the amount of uncertainty regard-ing the return that a financial asset will achieve over some period of time. Let's return to the share of common stock discussed in the previous paragraph. Let's suppose we are considering that share of stock at the beginning of the year when its price was $100 per share. And suppose further that we thought the stock probably would appreciate $10 over the course of the year and pay a $5 dividend. Based on these assumptions, the stock's most likely economic return in the coming year would be 15%. How-ever, let's say we were uncertain as to this outcome. There was a chance (let's say a one in four chance) that the stock would per-form worse, appreciating only $5 in value during the year and paying no dividend, and also a chance (again, say one in four) that the stock would appreciate by $15 dollars in the coming year and pay a $10 dividend. Figure 3 presents a graphic representa-tion of the financial risk of this hypothetical security: the predicted dispersion of possible economic returns on that security. The graph reveals the risk-return characteristics of this particular fi-

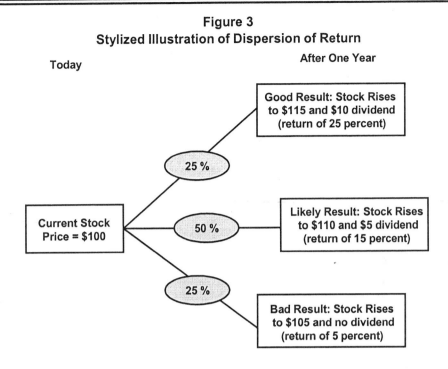

Figure 3
Stylized Illustration of Dispersion of Return

Today

After One Year

Current Stock Price = $100

25 %

Good Result: Stock Rises to $115 and $10 dividend (return of 25 percent)

50 %

Likely Result: Stock Rises to $110 and $5 dividend (return of 15 percent)

25 %

Bad Result: Stock Rises to $105 and no dividend (return of 5 percent)

nancial asset. The security has an expected return of 15% in the coming year, but its actual return could be as high as 25% or as low as 5%.

An important goal of financial analysis has been to document the risk-return characteristics of different kinds of financial assets — essentially trying to develop more realistic information about actual dispersions in economic returns that financial assets have achieved in the past. What empirical investigation of financial markets has discovered is that there is a strong and consistent relationship between the return on various classes of assets and the variation in the return (a.k.a. riskiness) of those assets. Government debt tends to have lower returns and lower risk (that is, variations in returns) than does corporate debt. Corporate debt, in turn, has lower returns and lower risk than corporate stock. And the stocks of larger, established corporations have lower returns and lower risk than the stocks of smaller, start-up firms. At least within the context of the U.S. capital markets in the last century, a wealth of empirical data support these relationships.

Figure 4, which is drawn from data collected by Ibbotson Associates for the 1926-2001 period, summarized the kind of analysis that financial economists have used to demonstrate the risk-return trade-off.

The first column of Figure 4 reports that average annual returns on various classes of financial assets during the 75 years between 1926 and 2000. As suggested above, stocks show the highest average returns, with large company stocks reporting average annual returns of 13.0% and small-company stocks showing an average annual return of 17.3%. The average returns are lower for long-term corporate bonds (6.0%), long-term government bonds (5.7%), intermediate-term government bonds (5.5%), and the U.S. Treasury bills (3.9%), which represent short-term government obligations.[14] U.S. Treasury bills represent an important benchmark in financial analysis, because they are considered to be a risk-free form of investment. Other financial assets are sometimes described in terms of the amount by which their returns exceed a risk-free rate of return. The second column in Figure 4, denominated risk premium, shows how much the average annual return on each asset class exceeded the average return on U.S. Treasury bills during the 1926-2001 period.

---

14. The last row in Figure 4 reports the average level of inflation in the United States during the 75 year period. This is an important number to bear in mind. The average rates of return for the other asset classes are reported in what's known as "nominal" terms, which includes both a "real" rate of return plus inflation. If a stock goes up in value by 10% in a year but inflation is 2%, then the real rate of return on the stock is approximately 8%. Although we tend to experience financial returns in nominal terms ("My stock portfolio went up twenty five percent last year!"), it is often more appropriate to focus on the real rate of return: an asset's expected rate of nominal return minus the expected rate of inflation. For example, if you wanted to know low long it would take for the real purchasing power of your portfolio to double, you would want to make that calculation based on the expected real rate of return of your portfolio. Using the Rule of 72, discussed above, if you thought the real rate of return on your portfolio were going to be 6%, then you would expect the purchasing value of that portfolio to double in 12 years.

Figure 4
Historical Performance of U.S. Financial Assets: 1926-2001

Asset Class	Average Annual Returns	Risk premium (relative to U.S. Treasury bills)	Standard Deviation of Annual Returns	Distribution of Annual Returns
Large-company stocks	13.0 %	9.1 %	20.2 %	
Small-company stocks	17.3 %	13.4 %	33.4 %	
Long-term corporate bonds	6.0 %	2.1 %	8.7 %	
Long-term government bonds	5.7 %	1.8 %	9.4 %	
Intermediate-term government bonds	5.5 %	1.6 %	5.8 %	
U.S. Treasury bills	3.9 %		3.2 %	
Inflation	3.2 %		4.4 %	

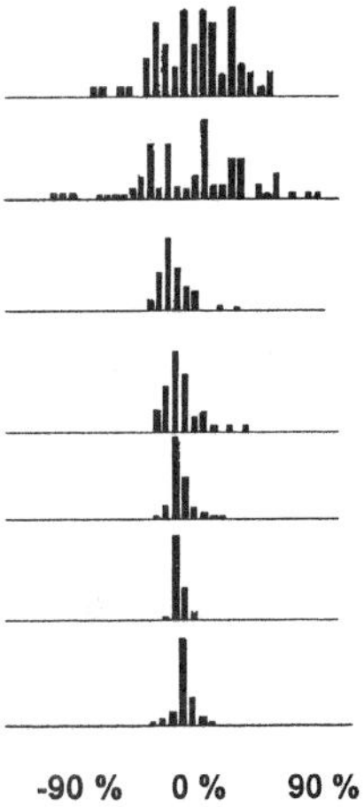

-90 %   0 %   90 %

Modified from *Stocks, Bonds, Bills and Inflation: 2001 Yearbook*, (Chicago: Ibbotson Associates, 2002).

The next two columns of Figure 4 offer two different perspectives on the financial risk — that is, variation in return — associated with each asset class. On the far right is a histogram plotting the distribution of annual returns for the asset class during the 75 year period of analysis. Notice that the returns on stocks are much more spread out than the returns on other asset classes, and that there have been a reasonably large number of years in which returns on stocks were negative. The column directly to the left of the histograms — "Standard Deviation of Average Annual Returns" — is a summary statistic that measures variation in annual returns. You'll learn more about standard deviations and how they are calculated in the courses on statistics, but for current purposes what is important to note is that the higher an asset class's average annual returns, the higher the variation in its annual returns. This fact is consistent with a basic premise of finance: that risk and return are positively correlated. The greater the return on an asset class, the greater the risk.

Practicing attorneys need not become experts in the intricacy of empirical studies into the historical performance of financial assets. But lawyers should know about the basic findings of this work, and also appreciate the way in which financial analysts employ this information to make predictions about the future and also to value investment opportunities today. A major premise of financial analysis is that future performance of financial assets will, to some degree, be comparable to past experience. Government securities are generally expected to yield lower returns than common stocks, but are also expected to generate less variation in return. The financial past is thus assumed to be prologue to the financial future. (But see Box 3.) Often times, it will fall to the attorney to remind his or her clients of the risk-return trade-off, and also to make sure that the client considers the implications of potential losses on assets, like investments in common stock, that have historically been associated with higher rates of return.

The Lawyer's Perspective

An important way in which lawyers make use of the risk-return trade-off is in helping clients avoid — or at least be adequately compensated for — potentially risky transactions. For example, suppose you represented a small bakery that was going to enter into a long-term contract to supply bread to a manufacturing firm and that the contract was going to require your client to make significant up-front investments (such as buying expensive new ovens). In addition to inspecting the counter-party's financial statements, you might also want to find out the interest rate that the manufacturing firm was paying on any bank loans or other outstanding debt. A high rate of interest would suggest that the firm was at above average risk of defaulting on its obligations. Accordingly, you might recommend that your client insist on an up-front payment to cover the cost of the new ovens, or at least a higher payment to compensate for the risks associated with entering into a long-term contract with the firm.

Box 3

Is the Past Really Prologue?

As explained in the text, financial analyses often proceed on the assumption that the past performance of financial assets – particularly the performance of common stock – is a good basis for predicting future returns, at least over extended periods of time such as ten years or more.   Within the academic community, however, there are growing concerns that traditional presentations of the risk-return trade-off may overstate the size of the equity premium (that is, amount by which average returns on common stock are expected to exceed average returns on other classes of financial assets). Some skeptics have expressed concern about drawing inferences about future stock market returns based solely on performance in the U.S. stock markets in the twentieth century. Arguably, our stock markets during this period were the most profitable of all time. Stock market returns in few if any other markets during the twentieth century performed as well, and many stock markets failed during the century. (How well over the long run do you think the average Russian investor did in the St. Petersburg stock market of 1900? Answer: very badly.) Predicting future returns from the U.S. twentieth-century experience is a bit like predicting future batting averages based on Barry Bonds's recent performance, or so some critics suggest.

C. The Value of Diversification

The value of diversification is another lesson from financial theory that lawyers should understand. This subject was first explored in Harry Markowitz, *Portfolio Selection* (1959). In essence, diversification offers investors a way of reducing the risk associated with particular investments without sacrificing return. You can think of diversification as a way of reducing (at least in part) the risk-return trade-off of some investments.

At root, the insight underlying diversification is that each individual investment has its own unique risks (again, meaning expected variation in return). Since these risks are unique, investors can offset the downside of some investments with the upside of other investments. This point can be illustrated if you think of the risks facing Suntan Lotion Co., a company that sells only suntan lotion, as compared with the risks facing Umbrellas Inc., a firm that manufactures only umbrellas. Sunny years are good for the former and bad for the latter, whereas rainy years are bad for the former and good for the latter. Normal weather means normal profitability for both firms. Figure 5 illustrates the hypothetical profits and losses that these two firms would earn across a series of years. When Suntan Lotion Co does well, Umbrellas Inc. does poorly and vice versa.

Figure 5
Profitability of Two Hypothetical Firms

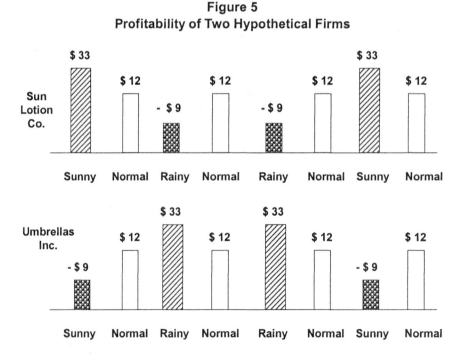

An investment solely in either Suntan Co. or Umbrellas Inc. will have a considerable amount of "weather" risk. For each firm, profits will vary from a $33 profit in good years and a $9 loss in bad years with an average $12 profit when the weather is normal. But imagine what would happen if you divided your investment evenly between the two firms — that is, if you diversified your investment across both firms. A portfolio divided evenly between the two investments will have no weather risk. In years with sunny weather, the extra profitability of Suntan Co. would exactly offset the losses on Umbrellas Inc. In years with rainy weather, the net effect would be the same but work in the other direction. With equal investments in both firms, you would obtain a consistent return in all years. In other words, you would have eliminated the expected variation in your return (a.k.a. risk).

Following up on the line of research inspired by Markowitz's early writings, financial analysts now tend to distinguish between diversifiable risk — that is, expected variations in return that can be eliminated through diversification — and nondiversifiable risk. The latter category of risks — nondiversifiable risk — is also sometimes called market risk or systematic risk. As these alternative formulations suggest, some financial risks are related to general market conditions or fluctuations in the larger economic system. Because variations in returns from these broader forces affect all investments (research suggests), these market risks cannot be eliminated through diversification.[15]

Again, lots of empirical evidence underlies portfolio theory, most of which is beyond the scope of this introductory coverage. To give readers a taste of the literature, we include Figure 6, which

---

15. Portfolio theory was largely developed through the analysis of U.S. financial markets. In the past decade, as financial markets have become more global, there has been considerable attention to the question of whether some U.S. market risk — hitherto thought to be nondiversifiable — might be reduced through diversification across national boundaries. Preliminary research suggests that this might be possible, at least to a limited degree; hence, our original understanding of nondiversifiable risk is beginning to change.

Figure 6
Gains from Diversification

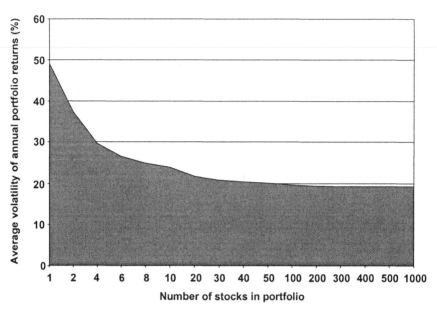

Source: Meir Statman, How Many Stocks Make a Diversified Portfolio, 22 J. Fin. & Quant. Anal. 353 (1987)

summarizes the variation in return of different-sized portfolios
of U.S. common stocks, as calculated in a study published in 1987.
As this figure indicates, if your portfolio consisted of just 1 stock
— that is, had no diversification — then the average annual variation in your return would be nearly 50%. If your portfolio were
evenly divided between just 2 securities, the average variation of
return for such a portfolio would decline to 37%, and with a diversified portfolio of 10 securities, the expected variation would
come down to 23%. Following the curve down to a diversified
portfolio of 30 securities, one finds expected variation would decline to under 21%, which is fairly close to the levels of expected
variation in fully diversified portfolios. (With 1,000 securities,
expected variation declines only a little bit further to 19.21%.)
For this reason, money managers are often satisfied that they have

achieved most of the gains from diversification if they divide their portfolios among at least 30 different investments.[16]

For practicing lawyers, portfolio diversification offers several important lessons. Most importantly, in many contexts, lawyers assist their clients in making investment decisions. Individual clients will need to allocate retirement savings. Charities will have endowments to invest. Fiduciaries will be responsible for the management of trust assets. Regardless of the particular client's preference for balancing risk and return, the client's lawyer should be prepared to advise the client on the benefits of maintaining a diversified portfolio. The alternative — holding a nondiversified portfolio — exposes the client to unnecessary risks.

Understanding the value of diversification is also important if you represent a business enterprise that has a large amount of business risk — like a start-up technology firm. When trying to attract potential investors for such clients, lawyers often find themselves trying to persuade these investors that, as long as they are diversified, the investors shouldn't worry about the unique risks of a particular firm — only its market risk.[17] The force of arguments of this sort explains why institutional investors in the United States have become increasingly willing to invest in start-up companies; as long as these investors put funds in a large enough number of start-ups, the unique risks of particular firms should wash out as a result of diversification. Similarly, regulatory officials have slowly come to appreciate the benefits of

---

16. One needs to be a bit careful about following this rule of thumb, as the full benefits of diversification will not be achieved if all 30 investments are from a single sector of the economy — say, the shrimp-fishing industry — because the unique risks of each firm will be closely associated with other firms in the portfolio. Also, some more recent research has suggested that additional diversification may have significant benefits.

17. The possible range of returns for a start-up company are not irrelevant to investors as the range of returns determines a company's expected return. As we will see when we get to the valuation section of this chapter, expected returns have a substantial impact of the valuation of companies.

diversification. Thirty years ago, many financial intermediaries, from pension plans to trust funds, were largely restricted to investing in lower-risk assets, such as investment-grade bonds and blue-chip stocks. Now these entities are often allowed to invest in a much broader category of assets, provided their holdings are fully diversified. Within the academic world, this development is generally thought to be desirable because it has increased the expected returns of financial intermediaries (do you see why?) and because it has brought new sources of capital to certain segments of the economy.

D. The Capital Asset Pricing Model

As explored in the previous section, the risk — that is, expected variation in return — associated with individual securities can be divided into diversifiable and nondiversifiable risk. For financial economists and well-advised investors, the critical component of a security's risk is its nondiversifiable risk. In many areas of finance, including the valuation of financial assets discussed later in this chapter, analysts need to estimate the nondiversifiable risk of a particular security, for example, the common stock of a company like GE or Intel. Financial economists have developed a number of different methods to provide such estimates, the most familiar of which is the Capital Asset Pricing Model or CAPM.

First proposed in a pair of articles by John Lintner and William Sharp in the mid-1960s, CAPM is another important and useful financial theory that builds upon the concepts discussed above. The CAPM is, at root, an explanation of how capital markets establish the price of financial assets, most importantly common stocks. The CAPM accepts the premise that diversifiable risk is unimportant because the risk can (by definition) be eliminated through diversification. The model then predicts that the return on a particular stock depends to a substantial degree on the extent to which the stock's return varies with respect to general market movements. The model then postulates that, by looking to the manner in which a particular company's stock has varied in relationship to the general market in the past, analysts can determine how capital markets will value the stock now and in the future.

A formal presentation of CAPM is beyond the scope of this text. For practicing attorneys, what's important to know about the CAPM is that this model is the means whereby financial analysts derive a measure — known as beta — that summarizes the relationship between an individual stock's movements and general market fluctuations. The stock of a company with a beta of 1.0 has had an average market risk. A stock with a beta of more than 1.0 has been more volatile than the market average — that is, its price has tended to go up more in strong markets and go down more in bad markets. Finally, a stock with a beta of less than 1.0 has been less volatile than the market average.[18] Within the financial world, beta is often used as a shorthand way of describing a company's market risk.

A detailed presentation of the theoretical dimensions of beta and the CAPM more generally is not possible here. Nor do we have time to explore a recent debate over whether the historical price movement of a company stock as compared to market fluctuations is an accurate predictor of future price movements, an implicit premise of the CAPM. (In brief, questions have been raised about the stability of this relationship, but the weight of authority still seems to support some relationship and hence the usefulness of betas derived from historical price movements.) In

---

18. More precisely, CAPM beta measures the relationship between the amount by which returns on particular security exceed a risk-free rate of return (for example, the return on Treasury bills) and the amount by which the overall market return exceeds the risk-free rate or return. Once a security's beta is calculated, an analyst can estimate the expected return on the security. For the quantitatively inclined, the formula for deriving the expected returns on a particular security with CAPM is:

Expected Returns = Risk-Free Return + Beta x (Market Return – Risk-Free Return).

addition, there is the complexity of determining which market's fluctuations should be used to determine a security's beta. Traditionally, betas have been derived by comparing individual stock prices to general movements of U.S. stock markets; however, it may be more appropriate to make the comparisons with respect to global stock markets or perhaps even some aggregate market of financial assets. Finally, a number of alternative asset pricing models have emerged in recent years that arguably do a better job of explaining the risk and return of particular securities. These and other related issues are explored in upper-level courses on corporate finance, particularly when taught in business school or economics department curricula.

What lawyers need to know is that the CAPM remains a popular technique for estimating the nondiversifiable risk (a.k.a. market risk) of individual stocks. Depending on the nature of their practice, lawyers will have varying degrees of exposure to the CAPM and its use in deriving betas. Lawyers working on Wall Street and in other financial centers might encounter the techniques on a daily basis. Others will deal with the concepts less frequently. Many lawyers do, however, get involved in advising clients who are making investment decisions. How should a client invest a 401(k) retirement savings plan? What should a charitable organization do with its cash reserves? What is an appropriate investment strategy for a school endowment? To help clients make decisions of this sort, lawyers need to have a basic appreciation of the risk-return trade-off and also the principles underlying CAPM and other models for estimating the risk-return characteristics of individual securities.

5. The Valuation of Assets

The valuation of assets is not, typically, the responsibility of attorneys (at least not attorneys acting as legal advisers). Lawyers are, however, often involved in transactions where other parties — whether financial analysts or investment bankers (an increasing number of whom have legal training) — are engaged in valuation exercises. Sometimes these transactions are purely business transactions, such as deciding how much to offer to purchase a firm in a takeover transaction or merger. But valuation can also be important in family law (in determining a fair division of marital property for a divorce settlement), in litigation (in calculating the amount of damages caused by wrongful disruption of business activities), or in a host of other legal contexts. Accordingly, lawyers will often find it useful to understand how valuation techniques work, at least in a general sense.

A. Contemporaneous Transactions Involving Substantially Similar Assets

Perhaps the simplest way to estimate the value of an asset is by reference to a recently established market price for an identical or substantially similar asset. For example, in establishing the value of 100 shares of IBM common stock contributed to a charity, a donor would typically look at the price at which the common stock traded on the New York Stock Exchange on the date of the donation. Since shares of IBM common stock are essentially fungible, the market price of IBM shares is generally accepted as a good estimate of the value of other shares of the security at the time the market price was established.

In other contexts, where similar but not identical assets have recently been sold, a comparable approach can be used. A good example arises in the underwriting procedures for residential mortgages — the loans that most Americans use to purchase their homes. Typically, lending institutions will have underwriting standards that specify that the value of the loan may not exceed a certain percentage — say 80% or 95% — of the market value of the property the loan is used to finance. To demonstrate compliance with these requirements, licensed appraisers typically estimate the value of particular properties by comparing the property in question to comparable properties that have recently been sold. So, to determine the value of a three-bedroom ranch house in Smallville, an appraiser would typically look at the price of similar houses in the same community. Adjustments are made to reflect differences in the comparables upon which the appraiser has relied (for example, in the number of bedrooms or quality of construction), and an estimated market value of the property of interest is thereby derived. Real estate attorneys would often work closely with appraisers in such procedures and might even suggest comparable properties to corroborate the proposed valuation of their client's property.

B. Market Valuation Estimates Derived from Financial Statements

When the asset to be valued is an enterprise for which financial statements are available, there are a number of valuation techniques that derive valuation estimates from elements of those statements. Such approaches might be useful if the asset to be valued were a business that was wholly-owned by two partners, and one of the partners wanted to buy out the other partner's interests, perhaps because the second partner wanted to retire or perhaps because the two had had a falling out. Since such a partnership would typically be privately held, there would be no public market in partnership interests from which a market price could be readily estimated. However, the firm might well have audited financial statements, from which financial analysts could estimate the firm's market value.

The most common techniques of this sort consist of identifying one element of the firm's financial statement and then ascertaining the relationship between that element and the market value of the entity. One example of this approach is based on the value of a firm's owners' equity as reported on the firm's balance sheet, sometimes referred to as the firm's "book value."[19] If it can be ascertained that within a particular industry a typical ratio of market value of a firm to its book value is 2 to 1, then an analyst can estimate the firm's market value once the analyst knows the book value of the firm. Another similarly motivated approach looks to the entity's income statement and draws inferences based on an assessment of price earnings multiples within the relevant industry.[20] With this information and an estimate of a company's current earnings, it is also possible to estimate the company's current market value.

Both of these approaches proceed on an assumption that there is a reasonably consistent relationship between market values and financial statement measures, at least within similar industries. So, for example, if the two-person partnership mentioned above consisted of a national chain of restaurants similar to those operated by Outback Steakhouse, Inc., then an analyst might look to information about the market-to-book value and price earnings multiples for Outback Steakhouse and other comparable public firms in order to make estimates of the market value of the firm being appraised.

C. Discounted Cash Flow Analysis

Discounted cash flow analysis is another, more flexible technique for valuing assets. At root, this approach is similar to the way we valued periodic payments on a lottery ticket earlier in this chapter. The analyst first figures out how much cash a proposed investment will generate in the future and then calculates the

---

19. Owners' equity consists of contributed capital plus retained earnings. See pages 6-7 above. As discussed in the Accounting chapter, there are a variety of reasons why accounting measures of owners' equity will not equal market value, including the reliance on historical values in accounting statements and the omission of many intangible assets and contingent liabilities.

20. Price earnings multiples or PE ratios are explained earlier on pages 54-56. In brief, the PE ratio is the ratio of the price of a company's shares of common stock to the company's earnings per share in the most recent accounting period.

present value of those cash payments using an appropriate discount rate. If the cost of making the investment is less than the present value of projected cash payments, then the investment is said to have a positive net present value and may be worth undertaking.

Discounted cash flow analysis is commonly used to value companies — either to estimate an appropriate price of the company's common stock or to value the entire company in the context of a takeover transaction or merger. In valuations of this sort, the analyst would typically begin by examining the firm's financial statements and, in particular, its summary of cash flows in order to determine the amount of cash that the firm has generated in recent years. Then, the analyst would have to make some predictions about how that level of cash flow is likely to increase (or decrease) in future years. Finally, the analyst would have to determine an appropriate discount rate to calculate a present value of these cash payments.

Often times, analysts would use CAPM or some comparable asset pricing model to derive this discount rate. Thus, for a firm in an industry with betas of 1.5 or higher, the analyst would use a relatively large discount rate, whereas for a firm in an industry with betas of less than 1, the analyst would use a lower discount rate. Within the logic of finance, this approach has intuitive appeal because a stream of cash flows from a risky industry (one with a high beta) should have a lower present value than a comparable stream of cash flows from a less risky industry (one with a lower beta). Do you understand why?

Figure 7 presents a schematic view of the hypothetical cash flows of the sort that an investment banker might project for a potential takeover target. Initially, the analyst predicts, the firm is projected to generate $50,000 of cash in year one and slightly more in year two. In year three, the firm is expected to be shut down for renovations, and as a result will require a cash infusion (negative cash flow) of $175,000 to cover renovation costs. Thereafter, the firm's cash flows are projected to jump up to $70,000

Figure 7
Projected Cash Flow for Projected Firm

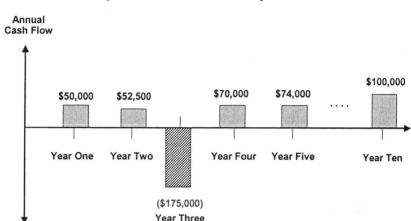

and continue to grow at a healthy rate, reaching $100,000 in year ten. Armed with these projections the analyst would then determine an appropriate discount rate of return for investments of this sort — perhaps relying on CAPM or some similar methodology — and then calculate a present value of these cash flows. That present value would suggest a plausible price for the takeover target. Obviously, projections and calculations of this sort require considerable expertise, if not clairvoyance, about industry trends and a host of other considerations, but for our purposes what is important to appreciate is the underlying logic of the valuation technique.

Once basic discounted cash flow analysis is completed along the line outlined above, analysts would commonly consider a wide range of alternative scenarios. For example, following up on the intuition of Coase's *Nature of Firm* article, the analyst might see if the value of the firm could be increased by selling off some assets or perhaps by making some additional investments in plant and equipment. The resulting change in cash flows for each new scenario would then be examined to determine if it enhanced firm value.

Box 4

Real Options and Valuation

An interesting recent extension of financial analysis is an approach known as real options. The approach combines aspects of decision analysis and traditional valuation techniques. Rather than valuing investment opportunities on the assumption that they will be undertaken on an all or nothing basis, real options analysis focuses on decision points in the future where decision-makers will have an option to abandon or continue the undertaking. In certain contexts – for example, when expensive investments can be postponed until the likelihood of a project's success will be clearer – real options analysis can uncover valuable investment opportunities where traditional discounted cash flow analysis would indicate an investment with low or even negative net present value. Real options might be useful to evaluate an investment in a new drug that would entail both an initial research phase and subsequent investment in expensive processing equipment. Particularly if the ultimate chances of success were low, expected returns on the drug might not warrant immediate investment in both the research and equipment. However, if the project were re-evaluated with a recognition that the decision to purchase processing equipment could be postponed until the research stage indicated whether there was a high likelihood that the drug would be successful, then the financial assessment of the project might well turn positive. Rather than valuing the overall project, the real option approach encourages analysts to consider whether the initial research is likely to generate a sufficiently valuable "option" to continue the project to the manufacturing phase.

Similar attention would be given to the financial structure of the target firm. Notwithstanding Modigliani & Miller's theoretical insights, financial analysts have long appreciated the tax advantages of debt financing. Accordingly, analysis might consider whether additional borrowings might lower the overall cost of capital for the firm, thereby decreasing the appropriate discount rate used to value the firm's cash flows and increasing the present value of the firm's projected cash flows.

While the details of discounted cash flow analysis are beyond the scope of this chapter, the basic principles of this foundational concept should be accessible to readers now. It is, in essence, simply a fancy application of the time value of money. There are three key questions: how much cash will the project in question produce in the future, when will that cash be generated, and what discount rate should be used to determine the present value of those cash flows. Everything else is detail.

For those who wish to pursue the concept of valuation further, we have appended to this chapter a Harvard Business School case study on the Eskimo Pie Corporation. In the case, the managers are trying to figure out how much the company is worth — that is, they are making a decision about valuation. The case includes much of the information necessary to apply many of the valuation methods described in this section. How much do you think this company is worth?

6. Suggestions for Further Reading

Students interested in the topics covered in this chapter can learn more about financial theory in the basic course on corporations as well as upper-level offerings in corporate finance, mergers and acquisitions, and securities regulation. Time-value-of-money issues are also treated in taxation courses, especially those focusing on the tax treatment of new financial instruments. More general questions of valuation are presented in a number of additional law school courses, such as family and employment law, although not always explicitly.

For those interested in exploring more technical aspects of finance, there are a number of good texts available. Stephen A. Ross, Randolph W. Westerfield, and Jeffery Jaffee, *Corporate Finance*, 6th ed. (Boston, MA: McGraw Hill College Division, 2003), offers a particularly clear presentation of the fundamentals of corporate finance. Another standard and slightly more challenging text is Behzad Razavi, Richard A. Brealey, and Stewart C. Meyers, *Principles of Corporate Finance*, 7th ed. (Boston, MA: McGraw Hill College Division, 2002). For those interested in a treatment that emphasizes option pricing theory, try Zvi Bodie and Robert C. Merton, *Finance* (Upper Saddle River, NJ: Prentice Hall, 1999). For a less technical treatment of the subject but a good overall introduction to the field, see Robert C. Higgins, *Analysis for Financial Management*, 6th ed. (Boston, MA: McGraw Hill/Irwin, 2001). For a critical overview of recent research on market efficiency, see Andrei Shleifer, *Inefficient Markets: An Introduction to Behavior Finance* (Oxford, UK: Oxford University Press, 2000).

Appendix 1:
Outback Steakhouse Financials
2002

2002
FINANCIAL REPORT

OUTBACK STEAKHOUSE, INC.

Table of Contents

Outback Steakhouse, Inc. and Affiliates
SELECTED FINANCIAL DATA
(Dollar amounts in thousands, except per share data)

Statements of Income Data(1):

	2002	2001	2000	1999	1998
Revenues					
Restaurant sales	$ 2,342,826	$ 2,107,290	$ 1,888,322	$ 1,632,720	$ 1,392,587
Other revenues	19,280	19,843	17,684	13,293	10,024
Total revenues	2,362,106	2,127,133	1,906,006	1,646,013	1,402,611
Costs and expenses					
Cost of sales	858,737	807,980	715,224	620,249	543,770
Labor and other related	572,229	507,824	450,879	387,006	327,261
Other restaurant operating	476,697	418,871	358,347	299,829	259,757
Depreciation and amortization	75,691	69,002	58,109	50,709	40,771
General & administrative expenses	89,868	80,365	75,550	61,173	52,879
Provision for impaired assets and restaurant closings	5,281	4,558	—	5,493	—
Contribution for "Dine Out for America"	—	7,000	—	—	—
Income from operations of unconsolidated affiliates	(6,180)	(4,517)	(2,457)	(1,089)	(514)
	2,072,323	1,891,083	1,655,652	1,423,370	1,223,924
Income from operations	289,783	236,050	250,354	222,643	178,687
Other income (expense), net	(3,322)	(2,287)	(1,918)	(3,042)	(850)
Interest income (expense), net	1,212	2,438	4,450	1,416	(1,357)
Income before elimination of minority partners' interest and provision for income taxes	287,673	236,201	252,886	221,017	176,480
Elimination of minority partners' interest	39,546	30,373	33,884	29,770	21,914
Income before provision for income taxes	248,127	205,828	219,002	191,247	154,566
Provision for income taxes	87,341	72,451	77,872	66,924	53,638
Income before cumulative effect of a change in accounting principle	160,786	133,377	141,130	124,323	100,928
Cumulative effect of a change in accounting principle (net of taxes)	(4,422)	—	—	—	(4,880)
Net income	$ 156,364	$ 133,377	$ 141,130	$ 124,323	$ 96,048
Basic earnings per common share					
Income before cumulative effect of a change in accounting principle	$ 2.10	$ 1.74	$ 1.82	$ 1.61	$ 1.33
Cumulative effect of a change in accounting principle (net of taxes)	(0.06)	—	—	—	(0.06)
Net income	$ 2.04	$ 1.74	$ 1.82	$ 1.61	$ 1.27
Diluted earnings per common share					
Income before cumulative effect of a change in accounting principle	$ 2.03	$ 1.70	$ 1.78	$ 1.57	$ 1.30
Cumulative effect of a change in accounting principle (net of taxes)	(0.06)	—	—	—	(0.06)
Net income	$ 1.97	$ 1.70	$ 1.78	$ 1.57	$ 1.24
Pro forma net income(2)				$ 122,398	$ 94,683
Pro forma basic earnings per common share(2)				$ 1.59	$ 1.25
Pro forma diluted earnings per common share(2)				$ 1.55	$ 1.22
Basic weighted average number of common shares outstanding	76,734	76,632	77,470	77,089	75,702
Diluted weighted average number of common shares outstanding	79,312	78,349	79,232	79,197	77,484
Balance Sheet Data:					
Working capital	$ 35,056	$ 16,600	$ 14,002	$ 12,276	$ 5,600
Total assets	$ 1,389,575	$ 1,237,748	$ 1,022,535	$ 852,282	$ 718,918
Long-term debt	$ 14,436	$ 13,830	$ 11,678	$ 1,519	$ 38,966
Interest of minority partners in consolidated partnerships	$ 41,488	$ 44,936	$ 16,840	$ 17,704	$ 9,912
Stockholders' equity	$ 1,052,976	$ 941,844	$ 807,590	$ 692,965	$ 548,440
Additional Selected Financial Data:					
System-wide sales	$ 2,910,000	$ 2,621,000	$ 2,329,000	$ 1,992,000	$ 1,668,000
Cash Dividends Per Share	$ 0.12	—	—	—	—

(1) All applicable share and per share data have been restated to reflect the retroactive effect of a three-for-two stock split effective on March 2, 1999.

(2) In 1999, the Company issued shares of its Common Stock for all of the outstanding shares of its New England franchisee which owned 17 Outback Steakhouses in Connecticut, Massachusetts, New Hampshire and Rhode Island. This merger was accounted for by the pooling-of-interests method using historical amounts and the amounts have been restated to give retroactive effect to the merger for all periods presented.

Management's Discussion and Analysis of Financial Condition and Results of Operations

INTRODUCTION

At December 31, 2002, Outback Steakhouse, Inc. and Affiliates (the "Company") restaurant system included the following:

Outback Steakhouse, Inc. and Affiliates	(Domestic) Outback Steakhouses	(International) Outback Steakhouses	Carrabba's Italian Grills	Fleming's Prime Steakhouses	Roy's	Lee Roy Selmon's	Bonefish Grills	Cheeseburger In Paradise	Total
Company owned	580	32	94	16	14	1	11	1	749
Development joint venture	3	9	29	-	1	-	1	-	43
Franchise	115	45	-	-	1	-	3	-	164
Total	698	86	123	16	16	1	15	1	956

Company owned restaurants include restaurants owned by partnerships in which the Company is a general partner. The partnership ownership interests in the restaurants range from 51% to 90%. The results of operations of Company owned restaurants are included in the consolidated operating results of the Company. The portion of income attributable to the minority interests is eliminated in the line item in the Company's Consolidated Statements of Income entitled "Elimination of minority partners' interest."

Development Joint Venture restaurants are organized as general partnerships in which the Company is one of two general partners and generally owns 50% of the partnership and its joint venture partner generally owns 50%. The restaurant manager of each restaurant owned by a Development Joint Venture purchases a 6% to 10% interest in the restaurant he or she manages. The Company is responsible for 50% of the costs of new restaurants operated as Development Joint Ventures and the Company's joint venture partner is responsible for the other 50%. The income derived from restaurants operated as Development Joint Ventures is presented in the line item "Income from operations of unconsolidated affiliates" in the Company's Consolidated Statements of Income.

The Company derives no direct income from operations of franchised restaurants other than initial franchise fees and royalties, which are included in the Company's "Other revenues."

Management's Discussion and Analysis of Financial Condition and Results of Operations

The following table sets forth, for the periods indicated: (i) the percentages which the items in the Company's Consolidated Statements of Income bear to total revenues or restaurant sales, as indicated; and (ii) selected operating data:

Statements Of Income Data:		Years Ended December 31,	
Revenues:	2002	2001	2000
Restaurant sales	99.2%	99.1%	99.1%
Other revenues	0.8	0.9	0.9
Total revenues	100.0	100.0	100.0
Costs and expenses:			
Cost of sales (1)	36.7	38.3	37.9
Labor and other related (1)	24.4	24.1	23.9
Other restaurant operating (1)	20.3	19.9	19.0
Depreciation and amortization	3.2	3.2	3.0
General and administrative	3.8	3.8	4.0
Provision for impaired assets and restaurant closings	0.2	0.2	—
Contribution for "Dine Out for America"	—	0.3	—
Income from operations of unconsolidated affiliates	(0.3)	(0.2)	(0.1)
Total costs and expenses	87.7	88.9	86.9
Income from operations	12.3	11.1	13.1
Other income (expense), net	(0.1)	(0.1)	(0.1)
Interest income (expense), net	0.1	0.1	0.2
Income before elimination of minority partners' interest and provision for income taxes	12.2	11.1	13.3
Elimination of minority partners' interest	1.7	1.4	1.8
Income before provision for income taxes	10.5	9.7	11.5
Provision for income taxes	3.7	3.4	4.1
Income before cumulative effect of a change in accounting principle	6.8	6.3	7.4
Cumulative effect of a change in accounting principle	(0.2)	—	—
Net income	6.6%	6.3%	7.4%

(1)   As a percentage of restaurant sales.

System-Wide Restaurant Sales (Millions Of Dollars):

	2002	2001	2000
Outback Steakhouses			
Company owned	$ 1,978	$ 1,848	$ 1,698
Domestic franchised and development joint venture	377	358	318
International franchised and development joint venture	88	81	75
	2,443	2,287	2,091
Carrabba's Italian Grills			
Company owned	253	204	169
Development joint venture	90	72	48
	343	276	217
Other			
Company owned	112	55	21
Franchised and development joint venture	12	3	—
	124	58	21
System-wide total	$ 2,910	$ 2,621	$ 2,329

4

Management's Discussion and Analysis of Financial Condition and Results of Operations

Fiscal Years Ended 2002, 2001 And 2000

Number Of Restaurants (At End Of Period):

	Years Ended December 31,		
	2002	**2001**	**2000**
Outback Steakhouses			
Company owned	612	575	521
Domestic franchised and development joint venture	118	114	103
International franchised and development joint venture	54	50	40
	784	739	664
Carrabba's Italian Grills			
Company owned	94	75	60
Development joint venture	29	28	21
	123	103	81
Fleming's Prime Steakhouse And Wine Bars			
Company owned	16	11	5
Roy's			
Company owned	14	11	3
Franchised and development joint venture	2	1	—
	16	12	3
Zazarac			
Company owned	—	—	1
Lee Roy Selmon's			
Company owned	1	1	1
Bonefish Grills			
Company owned	11	3	—
Franchised and development joint venture	4	1	—
	15	4	—
Cheeseburger In Paradise			
Company owned	1	—	—
System-Wide Total	956	870	755

Management's Discussion and Analysis of Financial Condition and Results of Operations

Fiscal Years Ended 2002, 2001 And 2000

None of the Company's individual brands are considered separate reportable segments for purposes of Statement of Financial Accounting Standards ("SFAS") No. 131; however, differences in certain operating ratios are discussed in this section to enhance the financial statement users' understanding of the Company's results of operations and its changes in financial condition.

Revenues.

Restaurant sales. Restaurant sales increased by 11.2% in 2002 as compared with 2001, and by 11.6% in 2001 as compared with 2000. The increases in 2002 and 2001 were primarily attributable to the opening of new restaurants. The following table summarizes additional activities that influenced the changes in restaurant sales at domestic Company owned restaurants for the years ended December 31, 2002, 2001 and 2000:

Average Unit Volumes:	2002	2001	2000
Restaurants opened for one year or more:			
Outback Steakhouses	$3,399,000	$3,444,000	$3,434,000
Carrabba's Italian Grills	$3,133,000	$3,067,000	$2,933,000
Restaurants opened for less than one year:			
Outback Steakhouses	$3,163,000	$2,855,000	$3,049,000
Carrabba's Italian Grills	$2,987,000	$3,387,000	$2,370,000
Operating Weeks:			
Outback Steakhouses	28,897	27,163	25,328
Carrabba's Italian Grills	4,221	3,428	3,031
Menu Price Increases:			
Outback Steakhouses	1.6%	2.8%	3.1%
Carrabba's Italian Grills	1.0%	4.5%	1.1%
Year To Year Same Store Percentage Change:			
Same-store sales (restaurants open 18 months or more):			
Outback Steakhouses	0.0%	0.8%	5.8%
Carrabba's Italian Grills	1.5%	7.0%	11.8%

Other Revenues. Other revenues, consisting primarily of initial franchise fees and royalties, decreased by $563,000 to $19,280,000 in 2002 as compared with $19,843,000 in 2001. The decrease was attributable to lower franchisee fees from international franchise operations partially offset by higher royalties from additional stores operated as franchises during 2002 compared with 2001. The decrease was also attributable to the Company's decision to allow international franchisees in certain markets, including Costa Rica, the Dominican Republic, Indonesia, Mexico, Malaysia, Singapore, Thailand, the United Kingdom and Venezuela to spend the royalties due to the Company on additional advertising to increase brand awareness and penetration in new markets. Other revenues increased by $2,159,000 to $19,843,000 in 2001 as compared with $17,684,000 in 2000. The increase was attributable to increased royalties and initial franchise fees from more stores opening and operating as franchisees of the Company both domestically and internationally during 2001 as compared with 2000.

6

Management's Discussion and Analysis of Financial Condition and Results of Operations

Fiscal Years Ended 2002, 2001 And 2000

Costs and expenses.

Cost of sales. Cost of sales, consisting of food and beverage costs, decreased by 1.6% of restaurant sales to 36.7% in 2002 as compared with 38.3% in 2001. The decrease was attributable to commodity cost decreases for beef, pork, dairy and seafood partially offset by higher produce costs. The decrease was also attributable to higher menu prices at both Outback Steakhouse and Carrabba's Italian Grills, and to an increase in the proportion of sales and cost of sales associated with the Company's non-Outback Steakhouse restaurants which operate at lower cost of goods sold levels than Outback Steakhouse. Cost of sales increased by 0.4% of restaurant sales to 38.3% in 2001 as compared with 37.9% in 2000. The increase was attributable to unfavorable commodity prices for beef and dairy products and was partially offset by menu price increases.

Labor and other related expenses. Labor and other related expenses include all direct and indirect labor costs incurred in operations. Labor and other related expenses increased as a percentage of restaurant sales by 0.3% to 24.4% in 2002 as compared with 24.1% in 2001. The increase resulted from higher employee health insurance costs, higher hourly employee bonuses, lower average unit volumes at Outback Steakhouse and an increase in the proportion of new restaurant formats which have higher average labor costs than domestic Outback Steakhouses and Carrabba's Italian Grills. Labor and other related expenses increased as a percentage of restaurant sales by 0.2% to 24.1% in 2001 as compared with 23.9% in 2000. The increase was attributable to higher hourly wage rates resulting from a competitive labor market, additional expenses related to enhanced employee health benefits and a new hourly employee bonus program.

Other restaurant operating expenses. Other restaurant operating expenses include all other unit-level operating costs, the major components of which are operating supplies, rent, repair and maintenance, advertising expenses, utilities, preopening costs and other occupancy costs. A substantial portion of these expenses are fixed or indirectly variable. Other operating expenses as a percentage of restaurant sales increased by 0.4% to 20.3% in 2002 as compared with 19.9% in 2001. The increase was attributable to higher insurance costs, lower average unit volumes for Outback Steakhouse and an increase in the proportion of new format restaurants and international Outback Steakhouses in operation which have higher average restaurant operating expenses as a percentage of restaurant sales than domestic Outback Steakhouses and Carrabba's Italian Grills. The increase was partially offset by lower restaurant preopening costs and lower natural gas costs as a percentage of restaurant sales during 2002 as compared with 2001. Other operating expenses as a percentage of restaurant sales increased by 0.9% to 19.9% in 2001 as compared with 19.0% in 2000. The increase was attributable to higher utility and natural gas prices and expenses associated with opening new restaurant formats. The increase was also attributable to an increase in the proportion of new format restaurants (primarily Fleming's Prime Steakhouse, Roy's, and Lee Roy Selmon's) and international Outback Steakhouses in operation, which have higher average restaurant operating expenses than domestic Outback Steakhouses and Carrabba's Italian Grills.

Depreciation and amortization. Depreciation and amortization costs were 3.2% of total revenues in both 2002 and 2001. The impact of reduced amortization expense due to the adoption of SFAS No. 142 "Goodwill and Other Intangible Assets" was offset by higher depreciation costs. The increase in depreciation costs primarily resulted from additional depreciation related to new unit development and to higher depreciation costs for new restaurant formats which have higher average construction costs than Outback Steakhouse and Carrabba's Italian Grills. Lower average unit volumes at Outback Steakhouse also contributed to depreciation costs increasing as a percentage of total revenues. Depreciation and amortization costs increased by 0.2% of total revenues to 3.2% in 2001, as compared with 3.0% in 2000. The increase primarily resulted from additional depreciation related to new unit development, "Take-away" room additions, new restaurant formats, which have higher than average construction costs than Outback Steakhouse and Carrabba's Italian Grills and additional amortization of goodwill associated with the purchase of ownership interests from certain minority partners, primarily area operating partners.

Management's Discussion and Analysis of Financial Condition and Results of Operations

Fiscal Years Ended 2002, 2001 And 2000

General and administrative. General and administrative expenses increased by $9,503,000 to $89,868,000 in 2002 as compared with $80,365,000 in 2001. The increase resulted from an increase in overall administrative costs associated with operating additional domestic and international Outback Steakhouses, Carrabba's Italian Grills, Fleming's Prime Steakhouses, Roy's and Bonefish Grills as well as costs associated with the development of new restaurant formats. General and administrative expenses increased by $4,815,000 to $80,365,000 in 2001 as compared with $75,550,000 in 2000. The increase resulted from higher overall administrative costs associated with operating additional Outback Steakhouses, Carrabba's, Fleming's Prime Steakhouses and Roy's as well as costs associated with the development of other new restaurant formats and other affiliated businesses.

Provision for impaired assets and restaurant closings. In accordance with SFAS No. 144, "Accounting for the Impairment of Long-Lived Assets," during 2002 the Company recorded a pre-tax charge to earnings of $5,281,000 which primarily is related to the closing of one Outback Steakhouse and one Roy's restaurant and to the reduction in the carrying value of three Outback Steakhouses and one Carrabba's Italian Grill. (Refer to Impairment of Long-Lived Assets measurement discussion in the Critical Accounting Policies section of Management's Discussion and Analysis of Financial Condition and Results of Operations.) In 2001, the Company recorded a pre-tax charge to earnings of $4,558,000 for the provision for impaired assets related to restaurant closings, severance and other associated costs. The provision related to the closing of three Outback Steakhouse and two Zazarac restaurants. (See Note 16 of Notes to Consolidated Financial Statements.) See "Liquidity and Capital Resources" for a discussion of the Company's expansion strategy.

Contribution for "Dine Out for America." This line item represents the Company's contribution of 100% of its sales proceeds from Thursday, October 11, 2001 to charitable organizations to benefit victims and families of victims of the terrorist attacks of September 11, 2001. The Company's sales on October 11, 2001 for the "Dine Out for America" fundraising event totaled approximately $7,000,000, all of which was contributed during 2001.

Income from operations of unconsolidated affiliates. Income from operations of unconsolidated affiliates represents the Company's portion of net income from restaurants operated as Development Joint Ventures. Income from Development Joint Ventures was $6,180,000 in 2002 as compared to $4,517,000 in 2001 and $2,457,000 in 2000. These increases primarily were attributable to additional stores operating as development joint ventures in each successive year and to an improvement in the operating results of these restaurants similar to that seen in the operating results of Company owned restaurants during 2002.

Income from operations. As a result of the increase in revenues, the changes in the relationship between revenues and expenses discussed above, the opening of new restaurants, the provision for impaired assets and restaurant closings in 2002 and 2001, and the 2001 "Dine Out for America" contribution, income from operations increased by $53,733,000 to $289,783,000 in 2002 as compared to $236,050,000 in 2001 and decreased by $14,304,000 to $236,050,000 in 2001, as compared with $250,354,000 in 2000.

Other income (expense), net. Other income (expense) represents the net of revenues and expenses from non-restaurant operations. Net other expense was $3,322,000 in 2002 compared with net other expense of $2,287,000 in 2001. The increase in the net expense primarily resulted from a decrease of approximately $1,580,000 in the cash surrender values of certain life insurance policies during 2002. The increase in net other expense is also attributable to the Company's portion of losses associated with the operation of Kentucky Speedway, and costs associated with a non-restaurant subsidiary; partially offset by a gain of approximately $500,000 on the sale of an airplane during 2002. Net other expense was $2,287,000 in 2001 compared with net other expense of $1,918,000 in 2000. The increase in the net expense resulted from a decrease in the cash surrender value of life insurance policies for key executives partially offset by the impact of the divestiture of a non-restaurant subsidiary.

8

Management's Discussion and Analysis of Financial Condition and Results of Operations

Fiscal Years Ended 2002, 2001 And 2000

Interest income (expense), net. Interest income was $1,212,000 in 2002 as compared with interest income of $2,438,000 in 2001 and interest income of $4,450,000 in 2000. The decrease in interest income resulted from lower interest rates on short term investments during 2002 compared with 2001 and 2000 offset by increased interest expense due to higher average debt balances on borrowings used to support Outback Steakhouse's international operations during 2002 compared with 2001 and 2000. The year-to-year changes in interest income resulted from changes in cash balances and short term interest rates, changes in borrowing needs as funds were expended to finance the construction of new restaurants and fluctuations in interest rates on the Company's lines of credit. (See Note 6 of Notes to Consolidated Financial Statements.)

Elimination of minority partners' interest. This item represents the portion of income or loss from operations included in consolidated operating results attributable to the ownership interests of minority partners. As a percentage of revenues, these allocations were 1.7%, 1.4%, and 1.8%, in 2002, 2001 and 2000, respectively. The ratio for 2002 increased by 0.3% of sales reflecting an increase in overall restaurant operating margins and improvements in new format restaurants, partially offset by a decrease in minority partners' ownership interests resulting from the purchase of minority interest in nine restaurants from area operating partners in 2002. The ratio for 2001 decreased by 0.4% of sales, reflecting a decrease in overall restaurant operating margins, the decrease in minority partners' ownership interests resulting from the purchase of minority interests in 55 restaurants from area operating partners in 2000 and early 2001 and the effect of the performance of new restaurant formats. (See Note 12 of Notes to Consolidated Financial Statements.)

Provision for income taxes. The provision for income taxes in all three years presented reflects expected income taxes due at the federal statutory rate and state income tax rates, net of the federal benefit. The effective tax rate was 35.2% in 2002, 35.2% in 2001 and 35.6% in 2000. The decrease in the effective tax rate between 2001 and 2000 resulted from tax savings associated with changes in the corporate state tax structure and an increase in FICA tip credits the Company was able to utilize in 2001. Approximately 44% of the Company's international restaurants in which the Company has a direct investment are owned through a Cayman Island corporation.

Cumulative effect of a change in accounting principle. The cumulative effect of a change in accounting principle represents the effect of the adoption of the transitional impairment provision of SFAS No. 142, "Goodwill and Other Intangible Assets." The adoption has been made effective as of the beginning of 2002. The cumulative effect of the change in accounting principle was approximately $4,422,000, net of taxes of approximately $2,199,000 during the year ended December 31, 2002. Basic and diluted earnings per share were both reduced by $0.06 due to the impact of the change in accounting principle.

Net income and earnings per common share. Net income for 2002 was $156,364,000, an increase of 17.2% over net income of $133,377,000 in 2001. Net income for 2001 was $133,377,000, a decrease of 5.5% over net income of $141,130,000 in 2000. Basic earnings per common share increased to $2.04 for 2002 from basic earnings per share of $1.74 in 2001. Diluted earnings per common share increased to $1.97 for 2002 from diluted earnings per common share of $1.70 in 2001. Basic earnings per common share decreased to $1.74 for 2001 from basic earnings per common share of $1.82 in 2000. Diluted earnings per common share decreased to $1.70 for 2001 from diluted earnings per common share of $1.78 in 2000.

Management's Discussion and Analysis of Financial Condition and Results of Operations

Liquidity and Capital Resources

The following table presents a summary of the Company's cash flows for the last three fiscal years (in thousands):

	2002	2001	2000
Net cash provided by operating activities	$ 338,060	$ 228,821	$ 239,546
Net cash used in investing activities	(168,066)	(233,662)	(145,819)
Net cash used in financing activities	(98,344)	(10,835)	(54,746)
Net increase (decrease) in cash	$ 71,650	$ (15,676)	$ 38,981

The Company requires capital principally for the development of new restaurants, remodeling older restaurants and investment in technology. The Company also requires capital to pay dividends to Common Stockholders (refer to additional discussion in the Dividend section of Management's Discussion and Analysis of Financial Condition and Results of Operations). Capital expenditures totaled approximately $181,798,000, $201,039,000 and $139,893,000 for the years ended December 31, 2002, 2001 and 2000, respectively. The Company either leases its restaurants under operating leases for periods ranging from five to thirty years (including renewal periods) or purchases free standing restaurants where it is cost effective. As of December 31, 2002, there were approximately 290 restaurants developed on land which was owned by the Company. (See Note 11 of Notes to Consolidated Financial Statements.) The Company also requires capital to repurchase the Company's Common Stock as part of an ongoing share repurchase program.

During 2001, the Company entered into an agreement with the founders of Bonefish Grill ("Bonefish") to develop and operate Bonefish restaurants. Under the terms of the Bonefish agreement, the Company purchased the Bonefish restaurant operating system for approximately $1,500,000. In addition, the interest in three existing Bonefish Grills was contributed to a partnership formed between the Bonefish founders and the Company, and, in exchange, the Company committed to the first $7,500,000 of future development costs of which approximately $5,031,000 had been expended as of December 31, 2002.

The Company entered into an agreement to develop and operate Fleming's Prime Steakhouse and Wine Bars ("Fleming's"). Under the terms of the Fleming's agreement, the Company purchased three existing Fleming's for $12,000,000 and committed to the first $13,000,000 of future development costs, all of which had been invested as of December 31, 2001.

During 1999, the Company entered into an agreement to develop and operate Roy's Restaurants. Under the terms of the Roy's agreement, the Company paid a consulting fee of approximately $1,800,000 to Roy Yamuguchi, founder of Roy's. Refer to the Debt Guarantees section of the Management's Discussion and Analysis of Financial Condition and Results of Operation.

The Company has formed joint ventures to develop Outback Steakhouses in Brazil and the Philippines. During the second quarter of 2001, the Company purchased three Outback Steakhouses in Puerto Rico which had been previously operated as franchises and will also develop future Company owned Outback Steakhouses in Puerto Rico. The Company is also developing Company owned restaurants internationally in Korea and Hong Kong.

In connection with the realignment of the Company's international operations, the Company expects to merge the interests of its franchisee operating restaurants in Japan into a new Japanese corporation which will be majority owned by the Company and which will have responsibility for the future development of Outback Steakhouse restaurants in Japan. As part of the realignment, the Company expects to become directly liable for the debt which it now guarantees, which totaled approximately $16,953,000, with a potential maximum of $20,000,000, as of December 31, 2002, referred to above and in Note 6 of Notes to Consolidated Financial Statements. As part of this transaction, the Company also expects to invest approximately $2,000,000 in equity in addition to the assumption of the bank debt.

Management's Discussion and Analysis of Financial Condition and Results of Operations

Long Term Debt

At December 31, 2002, the Company had two uncollateralized lines of credit totaling $140,000,000. Approximately $4,042,000 is committed for the issuance of letters of credit, of which $3,850,000 is required by insurance companies that underwrite the Company's workers compensation insurance. As of December 31, 2002, the Company had borrowed $10,000,000 on the line of credit to finance the development of new restaurants. The revolving line of credit contains certain restrictions and conditions as defined in the agreement which requires the Company to maintain net worth of $573,799,000 as of December 31, 2002, a fixed charge coverage ratio of 3.5 to 1.0, and a maximum total debt to EBITDA ratio of 2.0 to 1.0. At December 31, 2002, the Company was in compliance with all of the above debt covenants. See Note 6 of Notes to Consolidated Financial Statements.

The Company has notes payable with banks bearing interest at rates ranging from 6.5% to 6.75% to support the Company's Korean operations. As of December 31, 2002, the outstanding balance was approximately $16,353,000.

Debt Guarantees

The Company is the guarantor of two uncollateralized lines of credit that permit borrowing of up to $20,000,000 for its franchisee operating Outback Steakhouses in Japan. At December 31, 2002, the borrowings totaled approximately $16,953,000. See Note 11 of Notes to Consolidated Financial Statements.

The Company is the guarantor of an uncollateralized line of credit that permits borrowing of up to $35,000,000 for its franchisee operating Outback Steakhouses in California. At December 31, 2002, the outstanding balance on the line of credit was approximately $28,496,000.

The Company is the guarantor of an uncollateralized line of credit that permits borrowing of up to a maximum of $24,500,000 for its joint venture partner in the development of Roy's restaurants. At December 31, 2002, the outstanding balance was approximately $19,939,000.

The Company is the guarantor of bank loans made to certain franchises operating Outback Steakhouses. At December 31, 2002, the outstanding balance on the loans was approximately $195,000. No additional borrowing is permitted under these bank loans.

The Company is the guarantor of up to approximately $9,445,000 of a $68,000,000 note for Kentucky Speedway ("Speedway") in which the Company has a 22.2% equity interest and at which the Company operates catering and concession facilities. At December 31, 2002, the outstanding balance on the note was approximately $68,000,000. The Company's investment is included in the line item entitled "Investments In and Advances to Unconsolidated Affiliates." Speedway has not yet reached its operating break-even point. Accordingly, the Company has made two additional working capital contributions of $667,000 in December 2001 and $444,000 in July 2002, in addition to its original investment. The Company anticipates that it may need to make additional contributions for its pro rata portion of future losses, if any.

The Company is not aware of any non-compliance with the underlying terms of the borrowing agreements for which it provides a guarantee that would result in the Company having to perform in accordance with the terms of the guarantee.

Management's Discussion and Analysis of Financial Condition and Results of Operations

Other Material Commitments. The Company's contractual cash obligations, debt obligations, commitments and debt guarantees as of December 31, 2002, are summarized in the table below (in thousands):

Contractual Cash Obligations	Total	Payable During 2003	Payable 2004-2007	Payable After 2007
Operating leases..	$ 273,189	$ 45,091	$ 150,363	$ 77,735
Debt...	31,900	17,464	14,436	—
Commitments	2,469	2,469	—	—
Total contractual cash obligations	$ 307,558	$ 65,024	$ 164,799	$ 77,735
Debt Guarantees				
Debt guarantees	$ 89,140	$ 20,397	$ 60,479 (*) $	8,264
Amount outstanding under debt guarantees.................	$ 75,028	$ 17,350	$ 49,414	$ 8,264

(*) Includes approximately $250,000 maturing in 2006 and $278,000 maturing in 2007.

The Company expects that its working capital and capital expenditure requirements through the next 12 months will be met by cash flow from operations and, to the extent needed, advances on its credit line. (See Note 6 of Notes to Consolidated Financial Statements.)

Share Repurchase

On July 26, 2000, the Company's Board of Directors authorized a program to repurchase up to 4,000,000 shares of the Company's Common Stock. The timing, price, quantity and manner of the purchases will be made at the discretion of management and will depend upon market conditions. In addition, the Board of Directors also authorized a program to repurchase shares on a regular basis to offset shares issued as a result of stock option exercises. During the period from the program authorization date through December 31, 2002, approximately 3,005,000 shares of the Company's Common Stock have been issued as the result of stock option exercises. The Company will fund the repurchase program with available cash and bank credit facilities. As of December 31, 2002, under these authorizations the Company has repurchased approximately 5,880,000 shares of its Common Stock for approximately $161,514,000.

Dividends

On January 22, 2003, the Company's Board of Directors declared a quarterly dividend of $0.12 for each share of the Company's Common Stock. The dividend was paid March 7, 2003 to shareholders of record as of February 21, 2003. At the current dividend rate, the annual dividend payment is expected to be between $35,000,000 and $40,000,000 depending on the shares outstanding during the respective quarters. The Company intends to pay the dividend with cash flow from operations.

Critical Accounting Policies and Estimates.

The Company's discussion and analysis of its financial condition and results of operations are based upon the Company's consolidated financial statements, which have been prepared in accordance with accounting principles generally accepted in the United States of America. The preparation of these financial statements requires the Company to make estimates and judgments that affect the reported amounts of assets, liabilities, revenues and expenses, and related disclosure of contingent assets and liabilities during the reporting period (see Note 1 of Notes to Consolidated Financial Statements included in its Annual Report on Form 10-K). The Company bases its estimates on historical experience and on various other assumptions that are believed to be reasonable under the circumstances, the results of which form the basis for making judgments about the carrying value of assets and liabilities that are not readily apparent from other sources. Actual results may differ from these estimates under different assumptions or conditions. The Company's significant accounting policies are described in Note 1 of Notes to Consolidated Financial Statements included in its Annual Report on Form 10-K. The Company considers the following policies to be the most critical in understanding the judgments that are involved in preparing its financial statements.

Property, Fixtures and Equipment

Property, fixtures and equipment are recorded at cost. Depreciation is computed on the straight-line basis over the following estimated useful lives:

Buildings and building improvements	20 to 31.5 years
Furniture and fixtures	7 years
Equipment	2 to 15 years
Leasehold improvements	5 to 20 years

The Company's accounting policies regarding property, fixtures and equipment include certain management judgments and projections regarding the estimated useful lives of these assets and what constitutes increasing the value and useful life of existing assets. These estimates, judgments and projections may produce materially different amounts of depreciation expense than would be reported if different assumptions were used.

Impairment of Long-Lived Assets

The Company assesses the potential impairment of identifiable intangibles, long-lived assets and goodwill whenever events or changes in circumstances indicate that the carrying value may not be recoverable. In addition, on an annual basis the Company reviews the recoverability of goodwill. Recoverability of assets is measured by comparing the carrying value of the asset to the future cash flows expected to be generated by the asset. If the total future cash flows are less than the carrying amount of the asset, the carrying amount is written down to the estimated fair value, and a loss resulting from value impairment is recognized by a charge to earnings.

Judgments and estimates made by the Company related to the expected useful lives of long-lived assets are affected by factors such as changes in economic conditions and changes in operating performance. As the Company assesses the ongoing expected cash flows and carrying amounts of its long-lived assets, these factors could cause the Company to realize a material impairment charge.

Insurance Reserves

The Company self-insures a significant portion of expected losses under its workers compensation, general liability, health and property insurance programs. The Company purchases insurance for individual claims that exceed the amounts listed in the following table:

	2002	2003
Workers Compensation	$ 250,000	$ 1,000,000
General Liability	500,000	1,000,000
Health	230,000	250,000
Property damage	5,000,000	5,000,000

The Company records a liability for all unresolved claims and for an estimate of incurred but not reported claims at the anticipated cost to the Company based on estimates provided by a third party administrator and insurance company. The Company's accounting policies regarding insurance reserves include certain actuarial assumptions and management judgments regarding economic conditions, the frequency and severity of claims and claim development history and settlement practices. Unanticipated changes in these factors may produce materially different amounts of expense that would be reported under these programs.

13

Management's Discussion and Analysis of Financial Condition and Results of Operations

Revenue Recognition

The Company records revenues for normal recurring sales upon the performance of services. Revenues from the sales of franchises are recognized as income when the Company has substantially performed all of its material obligations under the franchise agreement. Continuing royalties, which are a percentage of net sales of franchised restaurants, are accrued as income when earned.

Unearned revenues primarily represent the Company's liability for gift certificates which have been sold but not yet redeemed and are recorded at the anticipated redemption value. When the gift certificates are redeemed, the Company recognizes restaurant sales and reduces the related deferred liability.

Principles of Consolidation

The consolidated financial statements include the accounts and operations of the Company and affiliated partnerships in which the Company is a general partner and owns a controlling interest. All material balances and transactions have been eliminated. The unconsolidated affiliates are accounted for using the equity method.

Outlook

The following discussion of the Company's future operating results and expansion strategy and other statements in this report that are not historical statements constitute forward-looking statements within the meaning of the Private Securities Litigation Reform Act of 1995. Forward-looking statements represent the Company's expectations or belief concerning future events and may be identified by words such as "believes," "anticipates," "expects," "plans," "should" and similar expressions. The Company's forward-looking statements are subject to risks and uncertainties that could cause actual results to differ materially from those stated or implied in the forward-looking statement. We have endeavored to identify the most significant factors that could cause actual results to differ materially from those stated or implied in the forward-looking statements in the section entitled "Cautionary Statement" on pages 16 and 17.

Future Operating Results

As of the date of this report substantial uncertainty exists as to the strength of consumer spending as a result of the economic downturn and conflict in the Middle East. The Company's revenue growth expectations summarized in the following paragraph assume that current spending trends do not worsen during 2003. The Company's revenues and financial results in 2003 could vary significantly depending upon consumer and business spending trends.

2003 Revenue. The Company plans to grow revenues in 2003 by opening additional restaurants and increasing comparable store sales and average unit volumes in all brands. The Company's expansion plans are summarized in this section. Based upon current economic conditions, the Company is currently planning for average unit volumes for Outback Steakhouse to increase by approximately 1% to 2% during 2003 compared with 2002. At present, the Company is not planning on any price increases during 2003 for Outback Steakhouse. However, the Company will reevaluate Outback menu pricing periodically and may change prices as economic and commodity conditions dictate. The Company is currently planning for average unit volumes for Carrabba's Italian Grills to increase by approximately 1% to 2% during 2003. The Company is not planning any price increases during 2003 for Carrabba's Italian Grills. However, the Company will reevaluate Carrabba's menu pricing periodically and may change prices as economic and commodity conditions dictate. The Company is also currently planning for average unit volumes to increase by approximately 1% to 2% for Fleming's Prime Steakhouse, 3% to 5% for Roy's and 1% to 2% for Bonefish Grill.

14

Management's Discussion and Analysis of Financial Condition and Results of Operations

Future Operating Results (continued)

2003 Cost of Sales. The Company is anticipating favorable pork rib and beef pricing versus 2002 and has also entered into contracts to secure its butter and cheese supplies for all of 2003 at a price that is slightly favorable to the average price in 2002. Cost of sales is also expected to decrease in 2003 as new format restaurants are developed that have a lower cost of sales as compared with Outback and Carrabba's. Cost of sales is expected to decrease as a percentage of restaurant sales in 2003 as a result of price increases taken in the latter part of 2002. The Company expects the favorable commodities and brand mix to be partially offset by unfavorable potato and onion pricing. Although the total change in food cost is subject to several factors, such as the mix of new restaurants, commodity availability and usage and price fluctuations in commodities for which the Company does not have purchase contracts, the current expectation for the Company is for a decrease of approximately 0.3% to 0.4% of sales for the full year.

2003 Labor Costs. During the last few years, the Company has experienced significant wage pressure resulting from a tight labor market. The Company expects this pressure to ease in 2003 as the labor market softens. The Company expects that as more of the new format restaurants (Roy's, Fleming's and Lee Roy Selmon's) are opened, that consolidated labor costs as a percentage of consolidated restaurant sales will increase because the labor costs as a percentage of sales at the new restaurant formats run at a higher rate than at Outback and Carrabba's. In addition, higher employee health insurance cost will also continue the upward pressure on labor costs as a percentage of restaurant sales. As a result, the Company is currently planning for its labor costs to increase by 0.1% to 0.2% of restaurant sales during 2003.

2003 Restaurant Operating Expenses. The Company plans to increase its advertising expenditures as a percent of sales in both Outback Steakhouse and Carrabba's Italian Grill in 2003. In addition, costs incurred prior to the opening of new restaurants are expected to increase as a result of additional restaurant openings in 2003 versus 2002. These preopening expenses total approximately $155,000 for each Company owned and joint venture Outback Steakhouse, approximately $190,000 for each Carrabba's Italian Grill, approximately $150,000 for each Bonefish Grill, and approximately $250,000 for each new Roy's and Fleming's Prime Steakhouse and Wine Bar. Restaurant operating expense ratios may vary materially from quarter to quarter depending on when new units open. As a result of the additional advertising expenditures and increase in planned openings of new restaurants, restaurant operating expenses may increase in 2003 by 0.3% to 0.4% of restaurant sales.

2003 Depreciation and Amortization. The Company expects depreciation costs, which are directly affected by investment in fixed assets, to increase as it builds new restaurants, improves and remodels existing restaurants and invests in technology. The Company estimates that its capital expenditures for the development of new restaurants will be approximately $175,000,000 to $200,000,000 in 2003.

2003 General and Administrative Expenses. Based upon its current plan, the Company expects that total general and administrative costs will increase by approximately 12% to 13% in 2003 compared with 2002.

Management's Discussion and Analysis of Financial Condition and Results of Operations

Expansion Strategy

The Company's goal is to add new restaurants to the system during 2003. The following table presents a summary of the expected restaurant openings for the full year 2003:

	2003
Outback Steakhouses – Domestic	
Company owned	26 to 28
Franchised or development joint venture	1 to 2
Outback Steakhouses – International	
Company owned	12 to 14
Franchised or development joint venture	2 to 3
Carrabba's Italian Grills	
Company owned	24 to 26
Fleming's Prime Steakhouse and Wine Bars	
Company owned	6 to 8
Roy's	
Company owned	1 to 2
Selmon's	
Company owned	1
Cheeseburger in Paradise	
Company owned	1 to 2
Bonefish Grill	
Company owned	15 to 18
Franchised or development joint venture	1 to 2

The Company estimates that its capital expenditures for the development of new restaurants will be approximately $175,000,000 to $200,000,000 in 2003 and intends to finance the development with cash flows from operations and the revolving line of credit referred to above. The Company anticipates that 60% to 70% of the Company owned restaurants to be opened in 2003 will be free standing units.

Cautionary Statement

The foregoing Management's Discussion and Analysis of Financial Condition and Results of Operations contains various "forward-looking statements" within the meaning of Section 27A of the Securities Exchange Act of 1933, as amended, and Section 21E of the Securities Exchange Act of 1934, as amended. Forward-looking statements represent the Company's expectations or beliefs concerning future events, including the following: any statements regarding future sales and gross profit percentages, any statements regarding the continuation of historical trends, and any statements regarding the sufficiency of the Company's cash balances and cash generated from operating and financing activities for the Company's future liquidity and capital resource needs. Without limiting the foregoing, the words "believes," "anticipates," "plans," "expects," "should," and similar expressions are intended to identify forward-looking statements.

Management's Discussion and Analysis of Financial Condition and Results of Operations

Cautionary Statement (continued)

The Company's actual results could differ materially from those stated or implied in the forward-looking statements included in the discussion of future operating results and expansion strategy and elsewhere in this report as a result, among other things, of the following:

(i)   The restaurant industry is a highly competitive industry with many well-established competitors;

(ii)   The Company's results can be impacted by changes in consumer tastes and the level of consumer acceptance of the Company's restaurant concepts; local, regional and national economic conditions; the seasonality of the Company's business; demographic trends; traffic patterns; consumer perception of food safety; employee availability; the cost of advertising and media; government actions and policies; inflation; and increases in various costs;

(iii)   The Company's ability to expand is dependent upon various factors such as the availability of attractive sites for new restaurants, ability to obtain appropriate real estate sites at acceptable prices, ability to obtain all required governmental permits including zoning approvals and liquor licenses on a timely basis, impact of government moratoriums or approval processes, which could result in significant delays, ability to obtain all necessary contractors and subcontractors, union activities such as picketing and hand billing which could delay construction, the ability to generate or borrow funds, the ability to negotiate suitable lease terms and the ability to recruit and train skilled management and restaurant employees;

(iv)   Price and availability of commodities, including, but not limited to, items such as beef, chicken, shrimp, pork, seafood, dairy, potatoes, onions and energy costs are subject to fluctuation and could increase or decrease more than the Company expects; and/or

(v)   Weather and other acts of God could result in construction delays and also adversely affect the results of one or more stores for an indeterminate amount of time.

Insurance
The Company purchases insurance for individual claims that exceed the amounts listed in the following table:

	2002	2003
Workers Compensation	$ 250,000	$ 1,000,000
General Liability	500,000	1,000,000
Health	230,000	250,000
Property damage	5,000,000	5,000,000

The Company records a liability for all unresolved claims at the anticipated cost to the Company at the end of the period based on the estimates provided by a third party administrator and insurance company.

Quantitative and Qualitative Disclosures about Market Risk

The Company is exposed to market risk from changes in interest rates on debt, changes in foreign currency exchange rates and changes in commodity prices.

The Company's exposure to interest rate risk relates to its $140,000,000 revolving lines of credit with its banks. Borrowings under the agreements bear interest at rates ranging from 57.5 to 95 basis points over the 30, 60, 90 or 180 London Interbank Offered Rate. At December 31, 2002 and 2001, the Company had a $10,000,000 outstanding balance on the lines of credit. The weighted average effective interest rate on the $10,000,000 outstanding balance was 2.39% at December 31, 2002.

Management's Discussion and Analysis of Financial Condition and Results of Operations

Quantitative and Qualitative Disclosures about Market Risk (continued)

The Company's exposure to foreign currency exchange risk relates primarily to its direct investment in restaurants in Korea, Hong Kong, the Philippines and Brazil and to its royalties from international franchisees in 21 countries. The Company does not use financial instruments to hedge foreign currency exchange rate changes.

Many of the food products purchased by the Company and its franchisees are affected by commodity pricing and are, therefore, subject to unpredictable price volatility. These commodities are generally purchased based upon market prices established with vendors. The purchase arrangement may contain contractual features that limit the price paid by establishing certain floors and caps. The Company does not use financial instruments to hedge commodity prices because the Company's purchase arrangements help control the ultimate cost paid. Extreme changes in commodity prices and/or long-term changes could affect the Company adversely. However, any changes in commodity prices would affect the Company's competitors at about the same time as the Company. The Company expects that in most cases increased commodity prices could be passed through to its consumers via increases in menu prices. From time to time, competitive circumstances could limit menu price flexibility, and in those cases margins would be negatively impacted by increased commodity prices.

This market risk discussion contains forward-looking statements. Actual results may differ materially from the discussion based upon general market conditions and changes in domestic and global financial markets.

Impact Of Inflation

The Company has not operated in a highly inflationary period and does not believe that inflation has had a material effect on sales or expenses during the last three years other than labor costs. The Company's restaurant operations are subject to federal and state minimum wage laws governing such matters as working conditions, overtime and tip credits. Significant numbers of the Company's food service and preparation personnel are paid at rates related to the federal minimum wage and, accordingly, increases in the minimum wage have increased the Company's labor costs in the last two years. To the extent permitted by competition, the Company has mitigated increased costs by increasing menu prices and may continue to do so if deemed necessary in future years.

18

Outback Steakhouse, Inc. and Affiliates

CONSOLIDATED BALANCE SHEETS
(In Thousands)

	December 31,	
ASSETS	**2002**	**2001**
Current Assets		
Cash and cash equivalents	$ 187,578	$ 115,928
Short term investments	20,576	20,310
Inventories	34,637	38,775
Other current assets	31,386	31,347
Total current assets	274,177	206,360
Property, fixtures and equipment, net	915,022	813,065
Investments in and advances to unconsolidated affiliates, net	38,667	46,485
Goodwill, net	85,842	80,074
Intangible assets, net	17,710	14,379
Other assets	58,157	77,385
	$ 1,389,575	$ 1,237,748
LIABILITIES AND STOCKHOLDERS' EQUITY		
Current Liabilities		
Accounts payable	$ 54,519	$ 47,179
Sales taxes payable	16,205	13,096
Accrued expenses	66,360	56,587
Unearned revenue	68,926	60,135
Income taxes payable	15,647	—
Current portion of long-term debt	17,464	12,763
Total current liabilities	239,121	189,760
Deferred income taxes	35,365	22,878
Long-term debt	14,436	13,830
Other long-term liabilities	6,189	24,500
Total liabilities	295,111	250,968
Commitments and contingencies (notes 6 and 11)		
Interest of minority partners in consolidated partnerships	41,488	44,936
Stockholders' Equity		
Common Stock, $0.01 par value, 200,000 shares authorized;		
78,750 and 78,554 shares issued; and 75,880 and 76,913 outstanding		
as of December 31, 2002 and 2001, respectively	788	786
Additional paid-in capital	236,226	220,648
Retained earnings	902,910	762,414
	1,139,924	983,848
Less Treasury Stock, 2,870 shares and 1,641 shares at December 31, 2002		
and 2001, respectively, at cost	(86,948)	(42,004)
Total stockholders' equity	1,052,976	941,844
	$ 1,389,575	$ 1,237,748

The accompanying notes are an integral part of these Consolidated Financial Statements.

Outback Steakhouse, Inc. and Affiliates

CONSOLIDATED STATEMENTS OF INCOME
(In Thousands, Except Per Share Amounts)

	Years Ended December 31,		
	2002	2001	2000
Revenues			
Restaurant sales	$ 2,342,826	$ 2,107,290	$ 1,888,322
Other revenues	19,280	19,843	17,684
Total revenues	2,362,106	2,127,133	1,906,006
Costs and expenses			
Cost of sales	858,737	807,980	715,224
Labor and other related	572,229	507,824	450,879
Other restaurant operating	476,697	418,871	358,347
Depreciation and amortization	75,691	69,002	58,109
General and administrative	89,868	80,365	75,550
Provision for impaired assets and restaurant closings	5,281	4,558	—
Contribution for "Dine Out for America"	—	7,000	—
Income from operations of unconsolidated affiliates	(6,180)	(4,517)	(2,457)
	2,072,323	1,891,083	1,655,652
Income from operations	289,783	236,050	250,354
Other income (expense), net	(3,322)	(2,287)	(1,918)
Interest income (expense), net	1,212	2,438	4,450
Income before elimination of minority partners'			
interest and provision for income taxes	287,673	236,201	252,886
Elimination of minority partners' interest	39,546	30,373	33,884
Income before provision for income taxes	248,127	205,828	219,002
Provision for income taxes	87,341	72,451	77,872
Income before cumulative effect of a change in accounting principle	160,786	133,377	141,130
Cumulative effect of a change in accounting principle (net of taxes)	(4,422)	—	—
Net income	$ 156,364	$ 133,377	$ 141,130
Basic Earnings Per Common Share			
Income before cumulative effect of a change in accounting principle	$ 2.10	$ 1.74	$ 1.82
Cumulative effect of a change in accounting principle (net of taxes)	(0.06)	—	—
Net income	$ 2.04	$ 1.74	$ 1.82
Basic weighted average number of common shares outstanding	76,734	76,632	77,470
Diluted Earnings Per Common Share			
Income before cumulative effect of a change in accounting principle	$ 2.03	$ 1.70	$ 1.78
Cumulative effect of a change in accounting principle	(0.06)	—	—
Net income	$ 1.97	$ 1.70	$ 1.78
Diluted weighted average number of common shares outstanding	79,312	78,349	79,232

The accompanying notes are an integral part of these Consolidated Financial Statements.

20

Outback Steakhouse, Inc. and Affiliates

CONSOLIDATED STATEMENTS OF STOCKHOLDERS' EQUITY
(In Thousands)

	Common Stock Shares	Common Stock Amount	Additional Paid-In Capital	Retained Earnings	Treasury Stock	Total
Balance, December 31, 1999	77,404	$ 775	$ 194,251	$ 501,384	$ (3,445)	$ 692,965
Issuance of Common Stock	995	10	20,290	—	—	20,300
Purchase of Treasury Stock	(1,980)	—	—	—	(48,615)	(48,615)
Reissuance of Treasury Stock	213	—	—	(4,131)	5,941	1,810
Net income...................................	—	—	—	141,130	—	141,130
Balance, December 31, 2000	76,632	785	214,541	638,383	(46,119)	807,590
Issuance of Common Stock	40	1	6,107	—	—	6,108
Purchase of Treasury Stock	(1,210)	—	—	—	(31,250)	(31,250)
Reissuance of Treasury Stock	1,451	—	—	(9,346)	35,365	26,019
Net income...................................	—	—	—	133,377	—	133,377
Balance, December 31, 2001	76,913	786	220,648	762,414	(42,004)	941,844
Issuance of Common Stock	196	2	15,578	—	—	15,580
Purchase of Treasury Stock	(2,691)	—	—	—	(81,650)	(81,650)
Reissuance of Treasury Stock	1,462	—	—	(6,767)	36,706	29,939
Dividends ($0.12 per share)..........	—	—	—	(9,101)	—	(9,101)
Net income...................................	—	—	—	156,364	—	156,364
Balance, December 31, 2002	75,880	$ 788	$ 236,226	$ 902,910	$ (86,948)	$ 1,052,976

The accompanying notes are an integral part of these Consolidated Financial Statements.

21

Outback Steakhouse, Inc. and Affiliates
CONSOLIDATED STATEMENTS OF CASH FLOWS (In Thousands)

	Years Ended December 31,		
Cash flows from operating activities:	**2002**	**2001**	**2000**
Net income	$ 156,364	$ 133,377	$ 141,130
Adjustments to reconcile net income to net cash provided by operating activities:			
Depreciation	73,288	62,712	52,946
Amortization	2,403	6,290	5,163
Provision for impaired assets and restaurant closings	5,281	4,558	—
Cumulative effect of a change in accounting principle	4,422	—	—
Minority partners' interest in consolidated partnerships' income	39,546	30,373	33,884
Income from operations of unconsolidated affiliates	(6,180)	(4,517)	(2,457)
Change in assets and liabilities:			
Decrease (increase) in inventories	4,138	(10,904)	(1,783)
(Increase) decrease in other current assets	(39)	(7,275)	1,928
Increase in goodwill, intangible assets and other assets	(6,064)	(7,378)	(34,265)
Increase in accounts payable, sales taxes payable and accrued expenses	20,222	21,033	21,052
Increase in unearned revenue	8,791	5,677	9,270
Increase (decrease) in income taxes payable	24,227	(13,621)	3,455
Increase in deferred income taxes	12,487	8,496	9,723
Decrease in other long-term liabilities	(826)	—	(500)
Net cash provided by operating activities	338,060	228,821	239,546
Cash flows from investing activities:			
Purchase of investment securities	(10,101)	(20,310)	—
Maturity of investment securities	9,835	—	—
Capital expenditures	(181,798)	(201,039)	(139,893)
Payments from unconsolidated affiliates	3,795	7,334	841
Distributions to unconsolidated affiliates	(7,626)	(5,264)	(2,707)
Investments in and advances to unconsolidated affiliates, net	17,829	(14,383)	(4,060)
Net cash used in investing activities	(168,066)	(233,662)	(145,819)
Cash flows from financing activities:			
Proceeds from issuance of Common Stock	—	—	13,315
Proceeds from issuance of long-term debt	6,511	20,329	15,400
Proceeds from minority partners' contributions	14,344	27,178	4,450
Distributions to minority partners	(55,966)	(42,739)	(39,198)
Repayments of long-term debt	(1,204)	(10,372)	(1,908)
Dividends paid	(9,101)	—	—
Payments for purchase of Treasury Stock	(81,650)	(31,250)	(48,615)
Proceeds from reissuance of Treasury Stock	28,722	26,019	1,810
Net cash used in financing activities	(98,344)	(10,835)	(54,746)
Net increase (decrease) in cash and cash equivalents	71,650	(15,676)	38,981
Cash and cash equivalents at the beginning of the year	115,928	131,604	92,623
Cash and cash equivalents at the end of the year	$ 187,578	$ 115,928	$ 131,604
Supplemental disclosures of cash flow information:			
Cash paid for interest	$ 1,457	$ 688	$ 215
Cash paid for income taxes	$ 42,958	$ 79,536	$ 68,095
Supplemental disclosures of non-cash items:			
Asset/liabilities of business transferred under contractual arrangements	$ (17,485)	$ 22,000	—
Purchase of minority partners' interest	$ 8,217	$ 13,608	$ 6,985

See Notes 5, 7, 10,12 and 13 for non-cash activity.

The accompanying notes are an integral part of these Consolidated Financial Statements.

NOTES TO CONSOLIDATED FINANCIAL STATEMENTS

1.   Summary of Significant Accounting Policies

Basis of Presentation - Outback Steakhouse, Inc. and Affiliates (the "Company") develops and operates casual dining restaurants primarily in the United States. The Company's restaurants are generally organized as partnerships, with the Company as the general partner.

Profits and losses of each partnership are shared based on respective partnership interest percentages, as are cash distributions and capital contributions with exceptions defined in the management agreement.

Additional Outback Steakhouse restaurants in which the Company has no direct investment are operated under franchise agreements.

Principles of Consolidation - The consolidated financial statements include the accounts and operations of the Company and affiliated partnerships in which the Company is a general partner and owns a controlling interest. All material balances and transactions between the consolidated entities have been eliminated.

The unconsolidated affiliates are accounted for using the equity method.

Reclassification - Certain prior year amounts shown in the accompanying consolidated financial statements have been reclassified to conform with the 2002 presentation. These reclassifications did not have any effect on total assets, total liabilities, stockholders' equity or net income.

Use of Estimates - The preparation of financial statements in conformity with generally accepted accounting principles requires management to make estimates and assumptions that affect the reported amounts of assets and liabilities and disclosure of contingent assets and liabilities at the date of the financial statements and the reported amounts of revenues and expenses during the reporting period. Actual results could differ from those estimated.

Cash and Cash Equivalents - Cash equivalents consist of investments which are readily convertible to cash with an original maturity date of three months or less.

Short term investments - The Company's short term investments, consisting primarily of high grade debt securities, are classified as held-to-maturity because the Company has the positive intent and ability to hold the securities to maturity. Held-to-maturity securities are stated at amortized cost, adjusted for amortization of premiums and accretion of discounts to maturity, which approximates fair value at December 31, 2002. The Company owns no investments that are considered to be available-for-sale or trading securities. At December 31, 2002, all held-to-maturity securities had maturities of less than one year and are classified as current assets.

Concentrations of Credit Risk - Financial instruments which potentially subject the Company to concentrations of credit risk are cash and cash equivalents, and short term investments. The Company attempts to limit its credit risk associated with cash and cash equivalents and short term investments by utilizing outside investment managers with major financial institutions that, in turn, invest in investment-grade commercial paper and other corporate obligations rated A or higher, certificates of deposit, government obligations and other highly rated investments and marketable securities. At times, cash balances may be in excess of FDIC insurance limits.

Inventories - Inventories consist of food and beverages, and are stated at the lower of cost (first-in, first-out) or market. The Company will periodically make advance purchases of various inventory items to ensure adequate supply or to obtain favorable pricing. At December 31, 2002 and 2001, inventories included advance purchases of approximately $10,499,000 and $17,003,000, respectively.

Goodwill - Goodwill represents the residual purchase price after allocation of the purchase price of assets acquired. On an annual basis, the Company reviews the recoverability of goodwill based primarily upon an analysis of discounted cash flows of the related investment asset as compared to the carrying value or whenever events or changes in circumstances indicate that the carrying amounts may not be recoverable.

Outback Steakhouse, Inc. and Affiliates

NOTES TO CONSOLIDATED FINANCIAL STATEMENTS

1. Summary of Significant Accounting Policies (continued)

Unearned revenue - Unearned revenues primarily represent the Company's liability for gift certificates which have been sold but not yet redeemed and are recorded at the anticipated redemption value. When gift certificates are redeemed, the Company recognizes restaurant sales and reduces the related deferred liability.

Property, fixtures and equipment - Property, fixtures and equipment are stated at cost, net of accumulated depreciation. Depreciation is computed on the straight-line method over the following estimated useful lives:

Buildings and building improvements.............. 20 to 31.5 years
Furniture and fixtures .... 7 years
Equipment .... 2 to 15 years
Leasehold improvements .... 5 to 20 years

Periodically, the Company evaluates the recoverability of the net carrying value of its property, fixtures and equipment by estimating its fair value which is generally measured by discounting expected future cash flows. The Company estimates fair value based on the best information available making the appropriate estimates, judgments and projections that are considered necessary. The fair value is compared to the carrying amount in the consolidated financial statements. A deficiency in fair value relative to the carrying amount is an indication of the need to reduce the carrying value of the assets. If the total of future undiscounted cash flows were less than the carrying amount of the property, fixtures and equipment, the carrying amount is written down to the estimated fair value, and a loss resulting from value impairment is recognized by a charge to earnings.

Construction in progress - The Company capitalizes all direct costs incurred to construct its restaurants. Upon opening, these costs are depreciated and charged to expense based upon their property classification. The amount of interest capitalized in connection with restaurant construction was approximately $290,000, $655,000 and $215,000 in 2002, 2001 and 2000, respectively.

Revenue Recognition - The Company records revenues from normal recurring sales upon the performance of services. Revenue from the sales of franchises are recognized as income when the Company has substantially performed all of its material obligations under the franchise agreement. Continuing royalties, which are a percentage of net sales of franchised restaurants, are accrued as income when earned.

Advertising Costs - The Company's policy is to report advertising costs as expenses in the year in which the costs are incurred. The total amounts charged to advertising expense were approximately $87,073,000, $72,686,000 and $68,993,000 in 2002, 2001 and 2000, respectively.

Income Taxes - The Company uses the asset and liability method which recognizes the amount of current and deferred taxes payable or refundable at the date of the financial statements as a result of all events that have been recognized in the consolidated financial statements as measured by the provisions of enacted tax laws.

The minority partners' interest in affiliated partnerships includes no provision or liability for income taxes as any tax liability related thereto is the responsibility of the individual minority partners.

24

Outback Steakhouse, Inc. and Affiliates

NOTES TO CONSOLIDATED FINANCIAL STATEMENTS

1.   Summary of Significant Accounting Policies (continued)

Stock Based Compensation - The Company accounts for stock based compensation under the intrinsic value method of accounting for stock based compensation and has disclosed pro forma net income and earnings per share amounts using the fair value based method prescribed by Statement of Financial Accounting Standards ("SFAS") No. 123, "Accounting for Stock Based Compensation." (See "Recently Issued Financial Accounting Standards" within this note.)

	Years Ended December 31,		
	2002	**2001**	**2000**
Net income, as reported	$ 156,364	$ 133,377	$ 141,130
Total stock-based employee compensation expense determined under fair value based method, net of related tax effects	(10,937)	(6,914)	(5,292)
Pro forma net income	$ 145,427	$ 126,463	$ 135,838
Earnings per common share:			
Basic-as reported	$ 2.04	$ 1.74	$ 1.82
Basic-pro forma	$ 1.90	$ 1.65	$ 1.75
Diluted as reported	$ 1.97	$ 1.70	$ 1.78
Diluted-pro forma	$ 1.83	$ 1.61	$ 1.71

The preceding pro forma results were calculated with the use of the Black Scholes option pricing model. The following assumptions were used for the years ended December 31, 2002, 2001 and 2000, respectively: (1) risk-free interest rates of 2.90%, 3.80%, and 5.03%; (2) dividend yield of 1.5%, 0.0% and 0.0%; (3) expected lives of 5.0 years, 3.5 years and 3.5 years; and (4) volatility of 32%, 33%, and 35%. Results may vary depending on the assumptions applied within the model. Compensation expense recognized in providing pro forma disclosures may not be representative of the effects on net income for future years.

Earnings Per Common Share - Earnings per common share are computed in accordance with SFAS No. 128, "Earnings Per Share," which requires companies to present basic earnings per share and diluted earnings per share. Basic earnings per share are computed by dividing net income by the weighted average number of shares of Common Stock outstanding during the year. Diluted earnings per common share are computed by dividing net income by the weighted average number of shares of Common Stock outstanding and dilutive options outstanding during the year.

Recently Issued Financial Accounting Standards

"Business Combinations" and "Goodwill and Other Intangible Assets"

On June 30, 2001, the Financial Accounting Standards Board ("FASB") finalized SFAS No. 141, "Business Combinations," and SFAS No. 142, "Goodwill and Other Intangible Assets." SFAS No. 141 requires all business combinations initiated after June 30, 2001, to be accounted for using the purchase method of accounting. With the adoption of SFAS No. 142 effective January 1, 2002, goodwill is no longer subject to amortization. Rather, goodwill will be subject to at least an annual assessment for impairment by applying a fair-value-based test. Under the new rules, an acquired intangible asset should be separately recognized if the benefit of the intangible asset is obtained through contractual or other legal rights, or if the intangible asset can be sold, transferred, licensed, rented, or exchanged regardless of the acquirer's intent to do so. These intangible assets will be required to be amortized over their useful lives. Generally, the Company performs its annual assessment for impairment during the third quarter of its fiscal year, unless facts and circumstances require differently.

Outback Steakhouse, Inc. and Affiliates

NOTES TO CONSOLIDATED FINANCIAL STATEMENTS

1. **Summary of Significant Accounting Policies (continued)**

Recently Issued Financial Accounting Standards (continued)

"Business Combinations" and "Goodwill and Other Intangible Assets"(continued)

In connection with the adoption of SFAS No. 142, the Company completed the transitional impairment testing of goodwill during the six months ended June 30, 2002. The adoption has been made effective as of the beginning of the Company's current fiscal year. In accordance with SFAS No. 142, goodwill was tested for impairment by comparing the fair value of our reporting units to their carrying value. Fair value was determined by the assessment of future discounted cash flows. The transitional impairment testing resulted in an initial goodwill impairment charge of approximately $4,422,000, net of taxes of approximately $2,199,000, during the six month period ended June 30, 2002. In accordance with SFAS No. 142, the initial impairment charge was recorded as a cumulative effect of a change in accounting principle in the Company's Consolidated Statements of Income for the six month period ended June 30, 2002.

The following table represents net income and earnings per share for prior periods had SFAS No. 142 been in effect for those periods (in thousands except per share data, unaudited):

	Years ended December 31,		
	2002	**2001**	**2000**
Reported income before cumulative effect of a change in accounting principle.......	$ 160,786	$ 133,377	$ 141,130
Add back: Goodwill amortization, net of taxes	—	3,954	3,229
Adjusted income before cumulative effect of a change in accounting principle	160,786	137,331	144,359
Cumulative effect of a change in accounting principle (net of taxes)	(4,422)	—	—
Adjusted net income..	$ 156,364	$ 137,331	$ 144,359
BASIC EARNINGS PER SHARE			
Reported income before cumulative effect of a change in accounting principle.......	$ 2.10	$ 1.74	$ 1.82
Add back: Goodwill amortization, net of taxes	—	0.05	0.04
Adjusted income before cumulative effect of a change in accounting principle	2.10	1.79	1.86
Cumulative effect of a change in accounting principle (net of taxes)	(0.06)	—	—
Adjusted net income..	$ 2.04	$ 1.79	$ 1.86
DILUTED EARNINGS PER SHARE			
Reported income before cumulative effect of a change in accounting principle.......	$ 2.03	$ 1.70	$ 1.78
Add back: Goodwill amortization, net of taxes	—	0.05	0.04
Adjusted income before cumulative effect of a change in accounting principle.......	2.03	1.75	1.82
Cumulative effect of a change in accounting principle (net of taxes)	(0.06)	—	—
Adjusted net income..	$ 1.97	$ 1.75	$ 1.82

"Accounting for Asset Retirement Obligations"

In June 2001, the FASB issued SFAS No. 143, "Accounting for Asset Retirement Obligations." SFAS No. 143 requires entities to record the fair value of a liability for an asset retirement obligation in the period in which it is incurred. Statement No. 143 is effective for fiscal years beginning after June 15, 2002, with earlier application encouraged. The Company does not expect the implementation of Statement No. 143 to have a material impact on its financial statements.

26

Outback Steakhouse, Inc. and Affiliates

NOTES TO CONSOLIDATED FINANCIAL STATEMENTS

1.   **Summary of Significant Accounting Policies (continued)**

Recently Issued Financial Accounting Standards (continued)

"Accounting for the Impairment or Disposal of Long-Lived Assets"

In August 2001, SFAS No. 144, "Accounting for the Impairment or Disposal of Long-Lived Assets," was issued, replacing SFAS No. 121, "Accounting for the Impairment of Long-Lived Assets and for Long-Lived Assets to Be Disposed Of," and portions of APB Opinion 30 "Reporting the Results of Operations." SFAS No. 144 provides a single accounting model for long-lived assets to be disposed of and changes the criteria that would have to be met to classify an asset as held-for-sale. SFAS No. 144 retains the requirement of APB Opinion 30 to report discontinued operations separately from continuing operations and extends that reporting to a component of an entity that either has been disposed of or is classified as held for sale. SFAS No. 144 is effective January 1, 2002, and was adopted by the Company as of that date. The adoption of SFAS No. 144 did not have a material impact on the Company's financial condition or results of operations in the year ended December 31, 2002.

"Accounting for Exit or Disposal Activities"

In June 2002, the FASB voted in favor of issuing SFAS No. 146 "Accounting for Exit or Disposal Activities." SFAS No. 146 addresses significant issues regarding the recognition, measurement and reporting of costs that are associated with exit and disposal activities, including restructuring activities that are currently accounted for pursuant to the guidance that the Emerging Issues Task Force (EITF) has set forth in EITF Issue No. 94-3, "Liability Recognition for Certain Employee Termination Benefits and Other Costs to Exit an Activity (including Certain Costs Incurred in a Restructuring)." The scope of SFAS No. 146 also includes: (1) costs related to terminating a contract that is not a capital lease and (2) termination benefits that employees who are involuntarily terminated receive under the terms of a one-time benefit arrangement that is not an ongoing benefit arrangement or an individual deferred-compensation contract. SFAS No. 146 is effective January 1, 2003. The Company does not expect the implementation of Statement No. 146 to have a material impact on its financial statements.

"Guarantor's Accounting and Disclosure Requirements for Guarantees, Including Indirect Guarantees of Indebtedness of Others"

In November 2002, the FASB issued Interpretation No. 45 (FIN 45), "Guarantor's Accounting and Disclosure Requirements for Guarantees, Including Indirect Guarantees of Indebtedness of Others." FIN 45 requires that upon the issuance of a guarantee, the guarantor must recognize a liability for the fair value of the obligation it assumes under the guarantee. FIN 45 provides that initial recognition and measurement should be applied on a prospective basis to guarantees issued or modified after December 31, 2002, irrespective of the guarantor's fiscal year end. The disclosure requirements are effective for financial statements of both interim and annual periods that end after December 15, 2002. The Company has complied with the disclosure requirements and is in the process of determining the impact, if any, of adopting the provisions for initial recognition and measurement for guarantees issued or modified after December 31, 2002.

Outback Steakhouse, Inc. and Affiliates

NOTES TO CONSOLIDATED FINANCIAL STATEMENTS

1.   Summary of Significant Accounting Policies (continued)

"Accounting for Stock-Based Compensation – Transition and Disclosure"

In December 2002, the FASB issued SFAS No.148, "Accounting for Stock-Based Compensation - Transition and Disclosure, an amendment of SFAS No. 123." This standard amends SFAS 123, "Accounting for Stock-Based Compensation," to provide alternative methods of transition for companies that voluntarily change to the fair value based method of accounting for stock-based employee compensation. It also requires prominent disclosure about the effects on reported net income of the company's accounting policy decisions with respect to stockbased employee compensation in both annual and interim financial statements. The transition provisions and annual disclosure requirements are effective for all fiscal years ending after Dec. 15, 2002, while the interim period disclosure requirements are effective for all interim periods beginning after Dec. 15, 2002. (See Stock Based Compensation discussion within this note.)

"Consolidation of Variable Interest Entities"

In January 2003, the FASB issued FASB Interpretation 46 (FIN 46), "Consolidation of Variable Interest Entities." This interpretation of Accounting Research Bulletin 51, "Consolidated Financial Statements," addresses consolidation by business enterprises of variable interest entities which possess certain characteristics. The interpretation requires that if a business enterprise has a controlling financial interest in a variable interest entity, the assets, liabilities, and results of the activities of the variable interest entity must be included in the consolidated financial statements with those of the business enterprise. This interpretation applies immediately to variable interest entities created after January 31, 2003 and to variable interest entities in which an enterprise obtains an interest after that date. Management believes that its accounting policies substantially comply with the provisions of FIN 46. Accordingly, adoption of FIN 46 is not expected to materially affect the Company's financial statements.

2.   Other Current Assets

Other current assets consisted of the following (in thousands):

	December 31,			
	2002		**2001**	
Deposits (including income tax deposits)	$	4,911	$	9,275
Accounts receivable		8,614		7,710
Accounts receivable – franchisees		2,920		3,560
Prepaid expenses		14,255		8,212
Other current assets		686		2,590
	$	31,386	$	31,347

28

Outback Steakhouse, Inc. and Affiliates

NOTES TO CONSOLIDATED FINANCIAL STATEMENTS

3. Property, Fixtures and Equipment, Net

Property, fixtures and equipment consisted of the following (in thousands):

	December 31,	
	2002	2001
Land	$ 166,600	$ 158,314
Buildings and building improvements	454,682	382,793
Furniture and fixtures	119,450	99,767
Equipment	295,718	238,285
Leasehold improvements	201,975	185,623
Construction in progress	30,992	35,464
Accumulated depreciation	(354,395)	(287,181)
	$ 915,022	$ 813,065

4. Goodwill and Intangible Assets, Net

Intangible assets consisted of the following (in thousands):

	December 31,	
	2002	2001
Non-compete/non-disclosure and related contractual agreements	$ 15,513	$ 10,141
Accumulated amortization	(6,657)	(4,482)
Liquor licenses	11,878	11,204
Accumulated amortization	(3,024)	(2,484)
	$ 17,710	$ 14,379

Aggregate amortization expense on the intangible assets subject to amortization was approximately $2,403,000 for 2002 and is estimated to be approximately $2,500,000 to $3,000,000 for each of the years ending December 31, 2003 through 2007.

The change in the carrying amount of goodwill for the year ended December 31, 2002 is as follows:

December 31, 2001	$ 80,074
Acquisitions	12,389
Transition impairment	(6,621)
December 31, 2002	$ 85,842

(See Note 1 of Notes to Consolidated Financial Statements.)

5. Other Assets

Other assets consisted of the following (in thousands):

	December 31,	
	2002	2001
Other assets	$ 43,157	$ 42,885
Assets of business transferred under contractual agreement	—	15,500
Deferred license fee	15,000	19,000
	$ 58,157	$ 77,385

Outback Steakhouse, Inc. and Affiliates

NOTES TO CONSOLIDATED FINANCIAL STATEMENTS

5. Other Assets (continued)

During January 2001, the Company entered into a ten year licensing agreement with an entity owned by minority interest owners of certain non-restaurant operations. The licensing agreement transferred the right and license to use certain assets of these non-restaurant operations. License fees payable over the term of the agreement total approximately $22,000,000.

During July 2002, the Company agreed to defer certain scheduled payments of approximately $1,500,000 for one year. Subsequently, during the third quarter of 2002, the licensee made a $325,000 payment towards this deferred amount. During the fourth quarter of 2002, the Company agreed to revise the remaining payment schedule. In addition, based upon the status of the renegotiated payment schedule, the Company provided for approximately $1,000,000 with respect to anticipated remaining amounts due under the licensing agreement.

During 2002, the licensee made additional payments towards amounts due under the licensing agreement. Accordingly, based upon meeting certain criteria pursuant to the applicable accounting provisions, the Company reduced the net book value of the assets subject to the licensing agreement with the deferred gain associated with the transaction. No gain has been recognized on the transaction and the remaining deferred gain associated with future licensing fees under the licensing agreement will not be recognized until such time as the amounts due under the licensing agreement are realized. (See Note 8 of Notes to Consolidated Financial Statements.)

During 1999, the Company entered into life insurance agreements for five officers whereby the Company pays the premiums on the policies held in trust for these individuals. The primary purpose of these agreements is to provide the officers' estates with liquidity in the event of the officers' death to avoid the need for the estate to liquidate its holdings of the Company's stock. The Company will recover the premiums it pays through policy withdrawals or proceeds from the policy benefits in the event of death. The Company has included the amount of its collateral interest in the policies in Other Assets.

Other Assets includes approximately $5,569,000 in principal and accrued interest on loans made to Fleming's Prime Steakhouse II, LLC ("FPSH II"), the operator of three unaffiliated Fleming's Prime Steakhouses, which the Company has agreed to purchase. The value of these restaurants approximates the Company's carrying value of the loan as of December 31, 2002. The Company and FPSH II have agreed that the conveyance of the restaurants to the Company will satisfy the outstanding balance. Subsequent to December 31, 2002, the restaurants have been conveyed to the Company.

Other Assets also includes approximately $10,059,000 in loans to its operating partner in the Outback/Fleming's, LLC for its partner's share of capital to build new restaurants required beyond the initial $13,000,000 contributed by the Company. The Company expects to continue to make advances to its operating partner for the construction of new restaurants. The carrying value of the loan is exceeded by the value of the partners' interest in the partnership.

6. Long-Term Debt

Long-term debt consisted of the following (in thousands):

	December 31,	
	2002	**2001**
Revolving line of credit, interest at 2.39% and 3.67% at December 31, 2002 and 2001, respectively ..	$ 10,000	$ 10,000
Other notes payable, uncollateralized, interest at rates ranging from 3.07% to 6.75%		
and 4.40% to 7.50% at December 31, 2002 and 2001, respectively	21,900	16,593
	31,900	26,593
Less current portion	17,464	12,763
Long-term debt	$ 14,436	$ 13,830

Outback Steakhouse, Inc. and Affiliates

NOTES TO CONSOLIDATED FINANCIAL STATEMENTS

5.   Other Assets (continued)

During January 2001, the Company entered into a ten year licensing agreement with an entity owned by minority interest owners of certain non-restaurant operations. The licensing agreement transferred the right and license to use certain assets of these non-restaurant operations. License fees payable over the term of the agreement total approximately $22,000,000.

During July 2002, the Company agreed to defer certain scheduled payments of approximately $1,500,000 for one year. Subsequently, during the third quarter of 2002, the licensee made a $325,000 payment towards this deferred amount. During the fourth quarter of 2002, the Company agreed to revise the remaining payment schedule. In addition, based upon the status of the renegotiated payment schedule, the Company provided for approximately $1,000,000 with respect to anticipated remaining amounts due under the licensing agreement.

During 2002, the licensee made additional payments towards amounts due under the licensing agreement. Accordingly, based upon meeting certain criteria pursuant to the applicable accounting provisions, the Company reduced the net book value of the assets subject to the licensing agreement with the deferred gain associated with the transaction. No gain has been recognized on the transaction and the remaining deferred gain associated with future licensing fees under the licensing agreement will not be recognized until such time as the amounts due under the licensing agreement are realized. (See Note 8 of Notes to Consolidated Financial Statements.)

During 1999, the Company entered into life insurance agreements for five officers whereby the Company pays the premiums on the policies held in trust for these individuals. The primary purpose of these agreements is to provide the officers' estates with liquidity in the event of the officers' death to avoid the need for the estate to liquidate its holdings of the Company's stock. The Company will recover the premiums it pays through policy withdrawals or proceeds from the policy benefits in the event of death. The Company has included the amount of its collateral interest in the policies in Other Assets.

Other Assets includes approximately $5,569,000 in principal and accrued interest on loans made to Fleming's Prime Steakhouse II, LLC ("FPSH II"), the operator of three unaffiliated Fleming's Prime Steakhouses, which the Company has agreed to purchase. The value of these restaurants approximates the Company's carrying value of the loan as of December 31, 2002. The Company and FPSH II have agreed that the conveyance of the restaurants to the Company will satisfy the outstanding balance. Subsequent to December 31, 2002, the restaurants have been conveyed to the Company.

Other Assets also includes approximately $10,059,000 in loans to its operating partner in the Outback/Fleming's, LLC for its partner's share of capital to build new restaurants required beyond the initial $13,000,000 contributed by the Company. The Company expects to continue to make advances to its operating partner for the construction of new restaurants. The carrying value of the loan is exceeded by the value of the partners' interest in the partnership.

6.   Long-Term Debt

Long-term debt consisted of the following (in thousands):

	December 31,	
	2002	**2001**
Revolving line of credit, interest at 2.39% and 3.67% at December 31, 2002 and 2001, respectively ..	$ 10,000	$ 10,000
Other notes payable, uncollateralized, interest at rates ranging from 3.07% to 6.75%		
and 4.40% to 7.50% at December 31, 2002 and 2001, respectively	21,900	16,593
	31,900	26,593
Less current portion	17,464	12,763
Long-term debt	$ 14,436	$ 13,830

Outback Steakhouse, Inc. and Affiliates

NOTES TO CONSOLIDATED FINANCIAL STATEMENTS

6.   Long-Term Debt (continued)

Debt and Debt Guarantee Summary

Debt Obligations	Total	Payable During 2003	Payable 2004-2007(*)	Payable After 2007
Debt	$ 31,900	$ 17,464	$ 14,436	—
Debt Guarantees				
Debt guarantees	$ 89,140	$ 20,397	$ 60,479	$ 8,264
Amount outstanding under debt guarantees	$ 75,028	$ 17,350	$ 49,414	$ 8,264

(*) Includes approximately $250,000 maturing in 2006 and $278,000 maturing in 2007.

7.   Accrued Expenses

Accrued expenses consisted of the following (in thousands):

	December 31,	
	2002	**2001**
Accrued payroll and other compensation	$ 22,110	$ 19,207
Accrued insurance	17,002	13,206
Accrued property taxes	8,361	6,970
Other accrued expenses	18,887	17,204
	$ 66,360	$ 56,587

8.   Other Long Term Liabilities

Other long term liabilities consisted of the following (in thousands):

	December 31,	
	2002	**2001**
Accrued insurance	$ 4,000	$ 4,000
Other deferred liability	2,189	20,500
	$ 6,189	$ 24,500

In January 2001, the Company entered into a ten year licensing agreement with an entity owned by minority interest owners of certain non-restaurant operations. The licensing agreement transferred the right and license to use certain assets of these non-restaurant operations. The Company has deferred the gain associated with the transaction until such time as the amounts due under the licensing agreement are realized. See Note 5 of Notes to Consolidated Financial Statements.

9.   Stockholders' Equity

During 2002, the Company repurchased 2,691,000 shares of its Common Stock, $.01 par value, for an aggregate purchase price of approximately $81,650,000. During 2001, the Company repurchased 1,210,000 shares of its Common Stock, $.01 par value, for an aggregate purchase price of approximately $31,250,000. Repurchased shares are carried as Treasury Stock on the Consolidated Balance Sheets and are recorded at cost. During 2002 and 2001, the Company reissued approximately 1,462,000 and 1,451,000 shares of Treasury Stock, respectively, that had a cost of approximately $36,706,000 and $35,365,000, respectively for exercises of stock options.

On October 23, 2002, the Company's Board of Directors declared the Company's first quarterly dividend of $0.12 per share of the Company's Common Stock. The dividend totaled approximately $9,101,000 and was paid on December 6, 2002 to the shareholders of record as of November 22, 2002.

NOTES TO CONSOLIDATED FINANCIAL STATEMENTS

10. Income Taxes

Provision for income taxes consisted of the following (in thousands):

	Years Ended December 31,		
	2002	**2001**	**2000**
Federal:			
Current	$ 67,566	$ 60,686	$ 63,606
Deferred	12,711	6,253	9,075
	80,277	66,939	72,681
State:			
Current	6,156	4,334	4,543
Deferred	908	1,178	648
	7,064	5,512	5,191
	$ 87,341	$ 72,451	$ 77,872

The Company's effective tax rate differs from the federal statutory rate for the following reasons:

Income taxes at federal statutory rate	35.0 %	35.0 %	35.0 %
State taxes, net of federal benefit	2.6	2.4	2.5
Federal income tax credits	(3.7)	(3.6)	(3.3)
Other, net	1.3	1.4	1.4
Total	35.2 %	35.2 %	35.6 %

The income tax effects of temporary differences that give rise to significant portions of deferred tax assets and liabilities are as follows:

	December 31,	
	2002	**2001**
Deferred Income Tax Assets (In Thousands):		
Insurance reserves	$ 6,581	$ 6,779
Accrued advertising expense	1,876	1,004
Intangibles	9,815	11,137
Other, net	3,648	3,537
	21,920	22,457
Deferred Income Tax Liabilities (In Thousands):		
Depreciation	57,285	45,335
	57,285	45,335
Net deferred tax liability	$ (35,365)	$ (22,878)

11. Commitments and Contingencies

Operating Leases - The Company leases restaurant and office facilities and certain equipment under operating leases having initial terms expiring between 2002 and 2016. The restaurant facility leases primarily have renewal clauses of five to 20 years exercisable at the option of the Company. Certain of these leases require the payment of contingent rentals based on a percentage of gross revenues, as defined by the terms of the applicable lease agreement. Total rental expense for the years ended December 31, 2002, 2001 and 2000 was approximately $44,137,000, $34,634,000 and $31,155,000, respectively, and included contingent rent of approximately $3,392,000, $2,999,000 and $3,220,000, respectively.

Outback Steakhouse, Inc. and Affiliates

NOTES TO CONSOLIDATED FINANCIAL STATEMENTS

11. Commitments and Contingencies (continued)

Future minimum lease payments on operating leases (including leases for restaurants scheduled to open in 2003), are as follows (in thousands):

2003	$ 45,091
2004	43,371
2005	40,834
2006	36,258
2007	29,900
Thereafter	77,735
Total minimum lease payments	$ 273,189

Development Costs - During 2001, the Company entered into an agreement with the founders of Bonefish Grill ("Bonefish") to develop and operate Bonefish restaurants. Under the terms of the Bonefish agreement, the Company purchased the Bonefish restaurant operating system for approximately $1,500,000. In addition, the interest in three existing Bonefish Grills was contributed to a partnership formed between the Bonefish founders and the Company, and in exchange, the Company committed to the first $7,500,000 of future development costs of which approximately $5,031,000 had been expended as of December 31, 2002.

Litigation - The Company is subject to legal proceedings claims and liabilities which arise in the ordinary course of business. In the opinion of management, the amount of the ultimate liability with respect to those actions will not materially affect the Company's financial position or results of operations and cash flows.

Insurance - The Company purchased insurance for individual claims that exceed the amounts listed in the following table:

	2002	2001	2000
Workers Compensation	$ 250,000	$ 250,000	$ 250,000
General Liability	500,000	250,000	250,000
Health	230,000	230,000	230,000
Property damage	5,000,000	15,000	15,000

The Company records a liability for all unresolved claims at the anticipated cost to the Company at the end of the period based on the estimates provided by a third party administrator and insurance company. The Company believes it has adequate reserves for all self insurance claims.

Guarantees - The Company guarantees debt owed to banks by some of its franchisees, joint venture partners and unconsolidated affiliates. The maximum amount guaranteed is approximately $89,140,000 with outstanding guaranteed amounts of approximately $75,028,000 at December 31, 2002. The Company would have to perform under the guarantees if the borrowers default under their respective loan agreements. The default would trigger a right for the Company to take over the borrower's franchise or partnership interest.

In connection with the realignment of the Company's international operations, the Company expects to merge the interests of its franchisee operating restaurants in Japan into a new Japanese corporation which will be majority owned by the Company and which will have responsibility for the future development of Outback Steakhouse restaurants in Japan. As part of the realignment, the Company expects to become directly liable for the debt which it now guarantees, which totaled approximately $16,953,000, with a potential maximum of $20,000,000, as of December 31, 2002, referred to above and in Note 6 of Notes to Consolidated Financial Statements. As part of this transaction, the Company also expects to invest approximately $2,000,000 in equity in addition to the assumption of the bank debt.

NOTES TO CONSOLIDATED FINANCIAL STATEMENTS

12.   Business Combinations

In April 2002, the Company exercised its option to convert its $5,300,000 preferred stock investment in its Hong Kong franchisee into ownership of three Outback Steakhouse restaurants formerly operated as franchises.   The acquisition was accounted for by the purchase method.

As part of the Company's realignment of its international operations, the Company issued approximately 196,000 shares of Common Stock in May 2002 to purchase the 20% interest in Outback Steakhouse International LP ("International") that it did not previously own.   The acquisition was accounted for by the purchase method and the related goodwill is included in the line item entitled "Goodwill" in the Company's Consolidated Balance Sheets.   In addition, primarily for tax purposes, approximately 50% of International's restaurants in which the Company has a direct investment are owned through a Cayman Island corporation.

During 2002, the Company issued approximately 43,000 shares of Common Stock to two area operating partners to acquire its interest in nine Outback Steakhouses in Ohio, Pennsylvania and Tennessee. The acquisitions were accounted for by the purchase method, and the related goodwill is included in the line item entitled "Goodwill" in the Company's Consolidated Balance Sheets.

During 2002, the Company acquired two franchised Roy's restaurants for approximately $4,650,000. The restaurants were franchised prior to the creation of the Roy's joint venture with the Company. The acquisition was accounted for by the purchase method, and the related goodwill is included in the line item entitled "Goodwill" in the Company's Consolidated Balance Sheets.

During 2001, the Company issued approximately 191,000 shares of Common Stock to four area operating partners for their interests in 22 Outback Steakhouses in New York, Ohio, Utah and Nevada and 9 Carrabba's Italian Grills in Georgia and North Carolina. The acquisitions were accounted for by the purchase method, and the related goodwill is included in the line item entitled "Goodwill" in the Company's Consolidated Balance Sheets.

During 2000, the Company issued approximately 273,000 shares of Common Stock to four area operating partners for their interests in 33 Outback Steakhouses in Arizona, New Mexico, Northern New Jersey, New York Metropolitan area, North Texas and Virginia. The acquisitions were accounted for by the purchase method, and the related goodwill is included in the line item entitled "Goodwill" in the Company's Consolidated Balance Sheets.

13.   Stock Option and Other Benefit Plans

The Company's Amended and Restated Stock Option Plan (the "Stock Option Plan") was approved by the shareholders of the Company in April 1992, and has subsequently been amended as deemed appropriate by the Company's Board of Directors or shareholders. There are currently 22,500,000 shares of the Company's Common Stock which may be issued and sold upon exercise of options under the Stock Option Plan. The term of options granted is determined by the Board of Directors and optionees generally vest in the options over a one to ten year period.

The purpose of the Stock Option Plan is to attract competent personnel, to provide long-term incentives to Directors and key employees, and to discourage employees from competing with the Company.

In 2002, the Company adopted the 2002 Managing Partner Stock Option Plan (the "MP Stock Option Plan") to provide for the issuance of options to Managing Partners and other key employees of the Company upon commencement of employment and to Managing Partners upon completion of the term of their employment agreements. No options may be granted under the MP Stock Option Plan to Directors or Officers of the Company or any of its subsidiaries or affiliated partnerships. The MP Stock Option Plan is administered by the Board of Directors. There are currently 7,500,000 shares of the Company's Common Stock which may be issued or sold upon exercise of options under the MP Stock Option Plan. The term of options granted under the MP Stock Option Plan is determined by the Board of Directors and generally ranges from ten years to fifteen years.

Options under the Stock Option Plan and the MP Stock Option Plan may be options which qualify under Section 422 of the Internal Revenue Code ("Incentive Stock Options") or options which do not qualify under Section 422 ("Nonqualified Options"). To date, the Company has only issued Nonqualified Options.

Outback Steakhouse, Inc. and Affiliates

NOTES TO CONSOLIDATED FINANCIAL STATEMENTS

13.   Stock Option and Other Benefit Plans (continued)

The exercise price for options granted under the Stock Option Plan generally cannot be less than the fair market value at the date of grant of the shares covered by the option. The exercise price of options granted under the MP Stock Option Plan is determined by using a three month weighted average stock price to eliminate the daily trading increases and decreases in the stock price. This averaging method may result in option grants under the MP Stock Option Plan that are above or below the closing price as of the exact grant date. The Company believes that the averaging of the price is a more fair method of determining fair market value for long term incentives. Compensation expense results if the exercise price of these options is less than the market price on the date of grant.

As of December 31, 2002, the Company had granted to employees of the Company a cumulative total of approximately 21,811,000 options (after forfeitures) under the Stock Option Plan to purchase the Company's Common Stock at prices ranging from $0.19 to $37.94 per share which was the fair market value at the time of each grant. As of December 31, 2002, the Company had granted to employees of the Company a cumulative total of approximately 2,020,000 options under the MP Stock Option Plan to purchase the Company's Common Stock at prices ranging from $29.39 to $36.89 per share. As of December 31, 2002, options for approximately 2,757,000 shares were exercisable in total under both of the Plans.

The remaining contractual life for options granted was approximately four to ten years, three to nine years and two to eight years for the options granted during 2002, 2001 and 2000, respectively.

Activity in the Company's Stock Option Plan was:

	Options	Weighted Average Exercise Price
Outstanding at December 31, 1999	11,062,775	$ 20.59
Granted	3,076,855	26.73
Exercised	(807,888)	14.03
Forfeited	(141,790)	24.57
Outstanding at December 31, 2000	13,189,952	22.93
Granted	2,803,547	26.87
Exercised	(1,293,405)	16.90
Forfeited	(249,350)	26.39
Outstanding at December 31, 2001	14,450,744	23.55
Granted	3,329,901	32.10
Exercised	(1,425,428)	20.22
Forfeited	(499,408)	26.65
Outstanding at December 31, 2002	15,855,809	$ 25.56

Tax benefits resulting from the exercise of non-qualified stock options reduced taxes currently payable by approximately $9,733,000, $6,142,000 and $3,290,000 in 2002, 2001 and 2000, respectively. The tax benefits are credited to additional paid-in capital.

The Company has a qualified defined contribution 401(K) plan covering substantially all full-time employees, except officers and certain highly compensated employees. Assets of this plan are held in trust for the sole benefit of the employees. The Company contributed approximately $922,000 and $829,000 to the 401(K) plan during plan years ended December 31, 2002 and 2001 respectively.

Outback Steakhouse, Inc. and Affiliates

NOTES TO CONSOLIDATED FINANCIAL STATEMENTS

14. Related Party Transactions

During 2001, Mr. Lee Roy Selmon, a member of the Board of Directors invested approximately $101,000 for a 10% interest in the operations of a Company owned restaurant, which bears his name and to which he is making a material image contribution.

The Company paid approximately $407,705, $493,000 and $478,000 during 2002, 2001 and 2000, respectively, for advertising and a private suite license agreement to a partnership in which two officers/directors are general partners.

A member of the Board of Directors owns a 10% interest in a limited partnership that owns and operates an Outback Steakhouse restaurant pursuant to a franchise agreement with Outback Steakhouse of Florida, Inc., a wholly owned subsidiary of Outback Steakhouse, Inc.

A member of the Board of Directors, through his wholly-owned corporation, has made investments in the aggregate amount of approximately $331,000 in seven limited partnerships that are parties to joint ventures that own and operate certain Carrabba's Italian Grill restaurants.

A member of the Board of Directors and named executive officer of the Company, has made investments in the aggregate amount of approximately $658,000 in 14 limited partnerships that are parties to joint ventures that own and operate either certain Carrabba's Italian Grill restaurants or Bonefish Grill restaurants.

15. Segment Reporting

In June 1997, the FASB issued SFAS No. 131, "Disclosures about Segments of an Enterprise and Related Information." The Company operates restaurants under seven brands that have similar investment criteria and economic and operating characteristics and are considered one reportable operating segment. Management does not believe that the Company has any material reporting segments.

16. Provision For Impaired Assets And Restaurant Closings

In 2002, the Company recorded a pre-tax charge to earnings of approximately $5,281,000 for the provision for impaired assets related to restaurant closings, severance and other associated costs. The provision related to the closings of one Outback and one Roy's restaurant and to the reduction of the carrying value of three Outback Steakhouses and one Carrabba's Italian Grill.

In 2001, the Company recorded a pre-tax charge to earnings of $4,558,000 for the provision for impaired assets related to restaurant closings, severance and other associated costs. The provision related to the closings of three Outback and two Zazarac restaurants.

Outback Steakhouse, Inc. and Affiliates

NOTES TO CONSOLIDATED FINANCIAL STATEMENTS

17.   Earnings Per Share

The following table represents the computation of basic and diluted earnings per common share as required by SFAS No. 128 "Earnings Per Share" (in thousands, except per share data):

	Years Ended December 31,		
	2002	**2001**	**2000**
Net income...	$ 156,364	$ 133,377	$ 141,130
Basic weighted average number of common shares outstanding	76,734	76,632	77,470
Basic earnings per common share	$ 2.04	$ 1.74	$ 1.82
Effect of dilutive stock options	2,578	1,717	1,762
Diluted weighted average number of common shares outstanding...........	79,312	78,349	79,232
Diluted earnings per common share	$ 1.97	$ 1.70	$ 1.78

Diluted earnings per common share excludes antidilutive stock options of approximately 1,809,000, 2,699,000 and 2,493,000 during 2002, 2001 and 2000 respectively.

18.   Subsequent Events

On January 22, 2003, the Company announced that its Board of Directors declared a quarterly dividend of $0.12 per share of the Company's Common Stock. The dividend was paid March 7, 2003 to shareholders of record as of February 21, 2003.

In January 2003, the Company, through its wholly owned subsidiary, Outback Steakhouse of Florida, Inc., a Florida corporation, agreed in principle to acquire four Outback Steakhouses from its franchisee operating in Manhattan and Long Island. In addition, the Company agreed to purchase one restaurant currently under construction.

In January 2003, the Company, through its wholly owned subsidiary, OS Prime, Inc., a Florida corporation, acquired two Fleming's Prime Steakhouses and Wine Bars ("Fleming's") from the founders of Fleming's pursuant to the asset purchase agreement dated October 1, 1999.

Outback Steakhouse, Inc. and Affiliates

NOTES TO CONSOLIDATED FINANCIAL STATEMENTS

19. Selected Quarterly Financial Data (unaudited)

The following table presents selected quarterly financial data for the periods indicated (in thousands, except per share data):

	2002			
	March 31,	**June 30,**	**September 30,**	**December 31,**
Revenues	$ 578,989	$ 596,200	$ 584,247	$ 602,670
Income from operations	74,315	76,431	65,095	73,942
Income before provision for income taxes	63,866	65,534	55,246	63,481
Income before change in accounting principle	41,385	42,466	35,799	41,136
Net income	36,963	42,466	35,799	41,136
Basic earnings per share				
Income before accounting change	0.54	0.55	0.47	0.54
Net income	0.48	0.55	0.47	0.54
Diluted earnings per share				
Income before accounting change	0.52	0.53	0.46	0.53
Net income	0.46	0.53	0.46	0.53

	2001			
	March 31,	**June 30,**	**September 30,**	**December 31,**
Revenues	$ 521,253	$ 538,844	$ 529,045	$ 537,991
Income from operations	67,865	63,855	45,368	58,962
Income before provision for income taxes	58,648	56,217	39,198	51,765
Net income	37,887	36,546	25,400	33,544
Basic earnings per share	0.50	0.48	0.33	0.44
Diluted earnings per share	0.49	0.47	0.32	0.43

Outback Steakhouse, Inc. and Affiliates

REPORT OF INDEPENDENT CERTIFIED PUBLIC ACCOUNTANTS

To the Board of Directors and Stockholders of Outback Steakhouse, Inc.

In our opinion, the accompanying consolidated balance sheets and the related consolidated statements of income, stockholders' equity and cash flows present fairly, in all material respects, the financial position of Outback Steakhouse, Inc. and its subsidiaries (the "Company") at December 31, 2002 and 2001, and the results of their operations and their cash flows for each of the three years in the period ended December 31, 2002 in conformity with accounting principles generally accepted in the United States of America. These financial statements are the responsibility of the Company's management; our responsibility is to express an opinion on these financial statements based on our audits. We conducted our audits of these statements in accordance with auditing standards generally accepted in the United States of America, which require that we plan and perform the audit to obtain reasonable assurance about whether the financial statements are free of material misstatement. An audit includes examining, on a test basis, evidence supporting the amounts and disclosures in the financial statements, assessing the accounting principles used and significant estimates made by management, and evaluating the overall financial statement presentation. We believe that our audits provide a reasonable basis for our opinion.

As discussed in Notes 1 and 4 to the consolidated financial statements, the Company adopted Statement of Financial Accounting Standards No. 142, "Goodwill and Other Intangible Assets," effective January 1, 2002.

PricewaterhouseCoopers LLP

Tampa, Florida
February 13, 2003

Outback Steakhouse, Inc. and Affiliates

MARKET FOR REGISTRANT'S COMMON EQUITY AND RELATED SHAREHOLDER MATTERS

On June 15, 2000, the Common Stock of the Company began trading on the New York Stock Exchange ("NYSE") under the symbol "OSI." Before June 15, 2000, the Common Stock of the Company was traded in the over-the-counter market and was quoted on the NASDAQ National Market System under the symbol "OSSI." The following table sets forth, for the fiscal years ended December 31, 2002 and 2001, the high and low per share prices of the Company's Common Stock as reported by the NYSE.

| | 2002 | | | 2001 | | |
	High	Low	Dividends Declared	High	Low	Dividends Declared
First Quarter	$37.96	$32.45	—	$27.80	$20.25	—
Second Quarter	39.80	33.50	—	32.00	24.01	—
Third Quarter	35.75	25.99	—	30.00	23.95	—
Fourth Quarter	36.09	24.90	$0.12	35.62	24.91	—

As of February 28, 2003, there were approximately 1,654 registered holders of record of the Company's Common Stock.

On October 23, 2002, the Company's Board of Directors declared a quarterly dividend of $0.12 for each share of the Company's Common Stock. Future dividend decisions will be based on and affected by a number of factors, including the operating results and financial requirements of the Company. See "Managements Discussion and Analysis of Financial Condition and Results of Operation – Liquidity and Capital Resources" for additional discussion regarding the Company's dividend payment.

Corporate Headquarters
Outback Steakhouse, Inc., 2202 North West Shore Boulevard, 5th Floor, Tampa, FL 33607.

Shareholder Information
Exchange: New York Stock Exchange
Listed Security: OSI Common Stock

Reports on Form 10-K
A copy of the Company's Annual Report to the Securities and Exchange Commission on Form 10-K will be furnished to any shareholder without charge upon written request. Address to Investor Relations Department at: Outback Steakhouse, Inc., 2202 North West Shore Boulevard, 5th Floor, Tampa, Florida 33607.

Stock Transfer Agent and Registrar
The Bank of New York, Stock Transfer Administration, 101 Barclay Street, Suite 12-W, New York, New York 10286. Requests for changes and updates in shareholder records can be made to the Bank of New York Customer Service Department at 800-524-4458.

Independent Accountants
PricewaterhouseCoopers LLP, Tampa, Florida.

Company News
The Company's news releases, including quarterly earnings announcements, are available through our Company Toll-Free Investor Hotline. To receive a faxed copy of recent news releases, call 1-877-733-6774. This service is available 24 hours a day, 7 days a week. For additional Company information, visit the Company's website at www.outback.com.

Annual Meeting
The Annual Meeting of Shareholders will be held on Wednesday, April 23, 2003 at 10:00 a.m. Eastern Daylight Savings Time at the a la Carte Event Pavilion, 4050-B Dana Shores Drive, Tampa, Florida 33634.

H A R V A R D | B U S I N E S S | S C H O O L

9-293-084
REV: AUGUST 30, 2001

RICHARD S. RUBACK

Eskimo Pie Corporation

In early 1991, Reynolds Metals, the makers of Aluminum Foil and other aluminum products, decided to sell its holding of Eskimo Pie, a marketer of branded frozen novelties. Reynolds had few interests outside its aluminum and packaging business, and the Eskimo Pie Corporation, with roughly $47 million in sales, accounted for less than 1% of Reynolds revenues. Reynolds planned to use the proceeds from the sale of Eskimo Pie to fund investments in its core aluminum business. Eskimo Pie was 84% owned by Reynolds Metals, and 4% owned by the Reynolds Foundation. The remaining 12% of the Eskimo Pie was held by various Reynolds family members and a small group of outside investors.

Goldman Sachs, a New York investment banking firm, was retained to assist with the sale of Eskimo Pie. Goldman estimated that the sale price of Eskimo Pie would be about 1.2 times 1990 sales, or about $57 million. Nestle Foods paid a comparable multiple for Drumstick, another ice cream novelty company, in 1990. Goldman organized an auction for Eskimo Pie, and Nestle was the highest of six bidders with a price of $61 million.

Mr. David Clark, President of Eskimo Pie Corporation, recognized that the sale of Eskimo Pie to Nestle would mean the end of its independence. Nestle was likely to consolidate its ice cream novelty businesses by eliminating Eskimo Pie's headquarters and management staff. He had struggled to find a way to keep the company independent since he first learned of the sale. But Clark had been unable to raise sufficient funds to purchase Eskimo Pie in a leveraged buyout, and the sale to Nestle seemed inevitable.

The Eskimo Pie Corporation

Background

Eskimo Pie, a chocolate covered bar of vanilla ice cream, was the first ice cream novelty. Its history appears on the Eskimo Pie box:

> *Genuine Eskimo Pie . . .*

293-084

One day working in a confectionery store to supplement his teaching income, Christian K. Nelson became puzzled by a little boy's indecision between a chocolate candy bar and a scoop of ice cream. When questioned, the freckle-faced boy replied, "I want 'em both but I only got a nickel."

With a clever hunch and a little ingenuity, Mr. Nelson found a way to combine the two ingredients in what would become America's first chocolate-covered ice cream bar. The little boy got his wish and Mr. Nelson founded a corporation on the success of the Eskimo Pie product.

Christian Nelson, age 27, began trying to make chocolate stick to ice cream in 1920 while operating an ice cream and confectionery store in Iowa. After months of experimentation, Nelson discovered that cocoa butter made the chocolate adhere to the ice cream. He introduced his product as the "I-Scream-Bar" in 1921. One year later, Mr. Nelson formed a partnership with Russell Stover and the product was renamed Eskimo Pie.

Because the lack of refrigeration made centralized production and distribution impossible, Eskimo Pie licensed rights to make and distribute the Eskimo Pie bar according to Mr. Nelson's recipe. By the spring of 1922, licenses had been sold to 2,700 manufacturers across the country. Sales were averaging one million Eskimo Pies a day and soared to two million a day by early summer. Russell Stover, Nelson's business partner, designed a tin foil wrapper which added to the product's glamour and provided a mechanism to collect royalties. U.S. Foil Company (which was later renamed Reynolds Metal Company) manufactured the printed wrappers around the clock to satisfy demand.

In spite of the popularity of Eskimo Pies, the Eskimo Pie Corporation was not financially successful. Eskimo Pie had difficulty collecting royalties both because the company lacked a reliable accounting system and because of patent infringers. By the summer of 1923, it was estimated that over a billion Eskimo Pies had been sold and yet the firm could not pay its debt of $100,000. Nelson sold Eskimo Pie to the U.S. Foil Company, and in 1924 Eskimo Pie Corporation became a subsidiary of U.S. Foil Company.[1] Nelson was paid a small fraction of a cent in royalties on every Eskimo Pie sold thereafter.

1991 Operations

Eskimo Pie had two lines of business in 1991. The first was the licensing of the Eskimo Pie brand products and the sublicensing of Welch's and Heath brand products. The second was a manufacturing operation that produced and distributed ingredients and packaging for the dairy industry. **Table A** presents the sales breakdown of these businesses. The company was also engaged in intensive research and product development efforts to extend its product lines. Eskimo Pie had a total of 130 employees.

---

[1] Stover sold his share for $30,000 in 1923. Stover went on to develop a nationwide candy business. After the sale of Eskimo Pie to U.S. Foil, Nelson was employed by Eskimo Pie and retired as a vice president in 1961. His significant inventions include the use of dry ice to store ice cream and machinery that automated the production of ice cream novelties. Mr. Nelson died on March 8, 1992 at the age of 98.

Table A   Sales by Business Line

	Year Ended December 31,		
Business	**1989**	**1990**	**1991**
Licensing			
Eskimo Pie	58%	59%	56%
Welch's and Heath[a]	14	14	24
Flavors, packaging and other	28	27	20

[a]Heath products included only in 1991.

Exhibit 1 presents Historical Financial Information for Eskimo Pie from 1987 to 1990, and **Exhibit 2** contains summary of Cash Flows from 1989 and 1990.

Licensing

Eskimo Pie granted exclusive territorial licenses for the manufacture, distribution, and sale of Eskimo Pie brand products through a national network of about 20 dairy product manufacturers. Eskimo's licensees agreed to maintain the strict quality standards, and Eskimo maintained the right to inspect all premises used for the manufacture and handling of Eskimo products. The licensees are Eskimo Pie's direct customers, and the top 10 licensees account for over 75% of revenues. Carnation was Eskimo Pie's largest licensee and manufacturer with territorial licenses to 11 western states.

Payment to Eskimo Pie by licensees was embedded in the price paid for ingredients and packaging supplied by Eskimo Pie rather than as a royalty payment based on units sold. If a licensee elected to use outside parties for certain ingredients and packaging, the licensee then paid Eskimo Pie a trademark license fee.

Eskimo Pie also sublicensed the manufacture and distribution of frozen novelties under established brand names of other food companies. Sublicensing had been an important component of Eskimo Pies strategy since 1975 when it developed the Nestle Crunch Bar and sublicensed its manufacture and distribution. Shortly after it acquired Carnation, Nestle terminated the sublicensing arrangement in 1986.

In 1991 Eskimo Pie licensed frozen novelties for Welch's and Leaf Incorporated, who owns the Heath brand name. Under the arrangements, Eskimo Pie had the exclusive authority to grant sublicenses for the manufacture and sale of these products similar to the way it did for its own Eskimo Pie brand products. Eskimo Pie purchased the base ingredients from the food companies and re-sold them, along with packaging, to sublicensees. Approximately 80% of the Eskimo Pie brand licensees were also licensees for Welch's and/or Heath products.

Eskimo Pie provided centralized marketing for Eskimo Pie, Welch's, and Heath brand products. The majority of marketing expenses were spent on retail advertising and promotions; the balance went to regional consumer promotions using television and coupon campaigns. One or more of the Company's Eskimo Pie brand products were found in 98% of all U.S. grocery stores, and Eskimo Pie enjoyed one of the highest consumer brand name recognition levels in the industry. **Exhibit 3** shows the distribution and market share of Eskimo Pie products (including Heath and Welch's) during the 1987-1991 period.

Manufacturing

Eskimo Pie operated three plants in the United States. These plants manufactured key ingredients and packaging used by licensees, such as the proprietary chocolate coating, *Midnite Sun*, that gave Eskimo Pie products their distinctive flavor. The plants also produced generic ingredients and packaging sold both to licensees and non-licensees in the dairy industry. The plants employ a total of 46 hourly workers at an average hourly wage of $10.06. The plants also employed 18 salaried employees.

Product Innovation

Eskimo Pie's new product program was successful: ten products introduced since 1987 were being actively marketed and sold in 1991. Eskimo Pie was the first to market a sugar free frozen dairy novelty bar made with NutraSweet and held a patent on that product's coating. The introduction of *Sugar Freedom Eskimo Pie* products in 1987 was largely responsible for the growth of Eskimo Pie's unit market share from 2.3% in 1987 to 5.3% in 1991. As of 1991, the *Sugar Freedom Eskimo Pie* products were leading the Eskimo Pie line. The company was also the first to introduce a fat-free frozen novelty product made with Simplesse, a patented fat substitute. By the end of 1991, Eskimo Pie was test marketing a fat free ice cream sandwich and expected to introduce a *Fat Freedom Eskimo Pie* line in the spring of 1992.

The Frozen Novelty Industry

The frozen novelty industry in 1991 was highly fragmented with over 400 brands representing sales of $1.3 billion. During the 1980's, major food companies such as General Foods, Mars, and Coca Cola entered the frozen novelties business. This transformed the industry's structure of low growth, little advertising, and few participants into a rapidly growing industry. Industry revenues went from $590 million in 1980 to $1.5 billion by 1987. The number of ice cream novelty brands, 100 in 1980, expanded to over 500 by 1987. Advertising expenditures increased from less than $2 million to $75 million per year during this period. **Exhibit 4** presents the frozen novelties sales trends.

By the late 1980's, the industry began to consolidate, with many of the larger companies exiting or significantly reducing their commitment to the frozen novelty business. By 1991, advertising expenditures had been reduced to about $25 million, and the market growth had slowed significantly. **Table B** shows the top five frozen novelties as ranked by unit market share in 1991.

Table B   1991 Leading Frozen Novelty Brands

Brand	Company	Unit Share
Popsicle	Unilever	7.6%
Klondike	Empire of Carolina	5.4
Eskimo Pie	Eskimo Pie	5.3
Snickers	Mars	4.8
Weight Watchers	H.J. Heinz	4.3

Nestle's Offer

Reynolds retained Goldman Sachs to sell Eskimo Pie because of its long-standing relationship with Reynolds and because it represented Nestle in its Drumstick acquisition. David Clark was directed to work with the Goldman Sachs team that arrived in April 1991 to prepare a sales strategy and the documentation required by buyers. Clark and his staff cooperated reluctantly, recognizing that Eskimo Pie would be unlikely to continue its 70 year history of operating as a stand-alone company in Richmond and that its corporate staff would be unlikely to retain their positions. **Exhibit 6** presents the projected income statements that Goldman collected.

Eskimo Pie's management and Wheat First Securities, a Richmond, Va. investment banking firm, formed a group to attempt a private buyout. This group obtained $20 million in credit and contributed another $15 million in equity, but the bid was rejected early on when higher offers came in. The buyout proposal could not secure additional financing because of the generally tight credit environment and the unpopularity of high yield debt financed LBOs. Also, Eskimo Pie could not use secured borrowing because the business was not asset intensive.

Goldman contacted several potential buyers. Many expressed interest but were concerned that Eskimo Pie's licensing approach to the business diverged from the more traditional integrated manufacturing and marketing approach. Reynolds received six offers for Eskimo Pie. Nestle Foods was the highest bidder at $61 million, and Reynolds began negotiating the specifics of the sale in mid-1991.

Negotiations between Reynolds and Nestle progressed slowly because of two complications. First, Nestle, a Swiss company, wanted to tailor the transaction to take advantage of its tax conditions. Second, Eskimo Pie discovered in the third quarter of 1991 that a small quantity of cleanup solvents, inks and oils were disposed of at its New Jersey plant. The company contacted the regulatory authorities, and conducted testing to determine the extent of any contamination. Although Eskimo Pie did not expect cleanup costs to exceed $300,000, Nestle remained cautious.

The Proposed Initial Public Offering

As the end of fiscal year 1991 approached, it was becoming apparent that Eskimo Pie was going to have a record year. Sales were higher than anticipated and operating margins had improved. In addition, Eskimo had also accumulated a $13 million cash reserve. David Clark contacted Wheat First again, searching for an alternative to the Nestle acquisition that would keep Eskimo Pie independent. Any solution would have to provide Reynolds with as much cash as the proposed acquisition.

Wheat First proposed the initial public offering of Reynolds' shares. Reynolds had dismissed this possibility early on, at the advice of Goldman Sachs. Goldman argued that a public offering would be worth less than a private sale because of the potential for synergies with an acquiring firm. The fact that Nestle, with its potential synergies in its Carnation and Drumstick units, had submitted the highest bid seem to confirm Goldman's reasoning. Wheat First, however, had two reasons to think that its initial public offering might yield more than the sale to Nestle. First, as **Exhibit 5** shows, the new issues market was hot, and the number of new issues and their dollar value soared. Second, Wheat First was working with an updated forecast, and it projected a more promising outlook. The forecasted 1991 net income in **Exhibit 6** is $2,893,000; actual results were going to be closer to $4,000,000. And forecasted sales in 1991 were projected at about $57 million; actual sales would be about $61 million. Capital expenditures were expected to be less than $1 million in 1992.

Wheat First proposed a two-step transaction. First, Eskimo Pie would pay out a $15 million or $4.52 per share special dividend. The $15 million dividend would be funded by the $13 million in cash that Eskimo Pie had accumulated and another $2 million in debt. The second step of the transaction was an initial public offering of up to 100% of the existing Eskimo Pie common shares. Wheat First suggested offering 3.3 million secondary shares with the option to offer 10-15% more shares. This "Green Shoe"[2] clause would provide cash to payoff the $2 million loan and provide over $2 million in working capital.

Wheat First estimated that the offering price would be between $14 and $16 a share. **Exhibit 7** shows the proceeds from the initial public offerings at the two offering prices. At $16 a share, the firm and Reynolds obtained more from the IPO than from the Nestle bid of $61 million. Furthermore, even at an offering price of $14, the IPO equalled the Nestle offer, without the complications and conditions that Nestle wanted to attach to its purchase of Eskimo Pie. **Exhibit 8** shows that price earnings ratios for comparable companies such as Ben & Jerry's and Dreyer's Grand Ice Cream were about 30x. The S&P 500 was trading at 25 X earning at the time.

Wheat First had not done business with Reynolds, and Goldman Sachs advised Reynolds Metals against the initial public offering. Goldman argued a deal with Nestle was more certain, and they remained skeptical that an initial offering could yield as much as the private sale. The sale to Nestle was likely to be closed soon, especially in light of the potential public offering. An initial public offering would take several months to complete, and Reynolds would risk changes in market conditions that would cool off the IPO market. Furthermore, an offering the size of the proposed Eskimo Pie deal would be one of Wheat First's largest. Wheat First and the management of Eskimo Pie stressed that with a public offering, the sale of Eskimo Pie by Reynolds would be made much easier, without complicated negotiations and compromises. In addition, an independent Eskimo Pie would stay in Richmond which allowed Reynolds to get liquidity while saving a local company and local jobs.

---

[2] A "Green Shoe" clause in an underwriting agreement provides the issuer the opportunity to issue additional shares for distribution.

Eskimo Pie Corporation 293-084

Exhibit 1 Historical Financial Information

	Year Ended December 31,			
	1987	1988	1989	1990
Income Statement Data (in thousands):				
Net sales[a]	$30,769	$36,695	$46,709	$47,198
Cost of goods sold	21,650	25,635	31,957	31,780
Gross profit[a]	9,119	11,060	14,752	15,418
Advertising and sales promotions	4,742	4,241	5,030	5,130
General and administrative	6,068	5,403	6,394	7,063
Operating income (loss)	(1,691)	1,416	3,328	3,225
Interest income	308	550	801	1,004
Interest expense	(88)	(107)	(88)	(67)
Other income (expense)-net[b]	1,738	(77)	(108)	(20)
Income taxes	96	729	1,511	1,616
Net income	$ 171	$ 1,053	$ 2,422	$ 2,526
Balance Sheet Data (in thousands):				
Cash	$ 5,550	$ 8,109	$10,723	$13,191
Working capital	9,342	11,107	10,830	$ 11,735
Total assets	20,857	23,006	26,159	29,518
Long-term debt	1,269	1,094	919	744
Stockholders' equity	16,162	17,215	18,215	19,496
Per Share Data:				
Weighted average number				
of common shares outstanding	3,316	3,316	3,316	3,316
Net income per share	$ 0.05	$ 0.32	$ 0.73	$ 0.76
Cash dividend per share	-	-	$ 0.40	$ 0.40

Source: Eskimo Pie Prospectus, p. 10.

[a]Beginning in 1991 the Company increased prices for products and assumed responsibility for advertising and sales promotion costs previously shared with licensees. This change in business practice accounts for approximately one-half of the increase in net sales for 1991 with a similar impact on 1991 gross profit.

[b]Includes the gain on sale of building of approximately $1,700,000 in 1987.

Exhibit 2   Cash Flow Summary

	Year Ended December 31,	
	1989	1990
Operating activities:		
Net income	$2,422	$2,526
Depreciation	1,006	1,352
Amortization	175	118
Deferred income taxes	250	(58)
Pension liability and other	(154)	(156)
Decrease (increase) in receivables	1,212	(734)
Decrease (increase) in inventories and prepaid expenses	(524)	(51)
Increase (decrease) in payables to parent	2,054	(621)
Increase (decrease) in accounts payable and accrued expenses	143	3,006
Net cash provided by operating activities	6,595	5,382
Investing activities		
Capital expenditures[a]	(2,358)	(1,311)
Other	(121)	(101
Net cash used in investing activities	(2,479)	(1,412)
Financing activities		
Cash dividends	(1,327)	(1,327)
Principal payments on long-term debt	(175)	(175)
Net cash used in financing activities	(1,502)	(1,502)
Increase (decrease) in cash and cash equivalents	2,614	2,468
Cash and cash equivalents at beginning of year	8,109	10,723
Cash and cash equivalents at end of year	$10,723	$13,191

Source: Eskimo Pie Prospectus, p. F-4.

[a]Capital expenditures in 1989 are principally related to equipment acquired for use by licensees and, in 1990, an expansion of an ingredients manufacturing facility.

Eskimo Pie Corporation   293-084

Exhibit 3   Distribution and Market Share of Eskimo Pie, Heath, and Welch's Frozen Novelties

	1987	1988	1989	1990	1991
Distribution of at least one Eskimo product at U.S. Grocery Stores	76.3%	78.1%	91.2%	95.6%	97.9%
Unit Market Share of Eskimo products	3.3	3.9	5.7	6.8	7.5

Source: Eskimo Pie Prospectus

Exhibit 4   Industry Information for Frozen Novelties

Year	Industry Revenues (millions)	Units Sold (millions)	% Change in Sales	Average Price	Advertising Spending (millions)
1980	$590	N/A	N/A	N/A	$ 2
1981	680	N/A	15.3%	N/A	4
1982	770	457	13.2	$1.69	17
1983	940	525	22.1	1.79	23
1984	1,100	577	17.0	1.90	32
1985	1,300	643	18.2	2.02	44
1986	1,400	681	7.7	2.06	77
1987	1,500	717	7.1	2.09	38
1988	1,355	637	-9.7	2.13	26
1989	1,332	623	-1.7	2.19	40
1990	1,321	590	-0.8	2.24	21

Source: 1980-87 Nieldsen; 1988-90 IRI

293-084   -10-

Exhibit 5   Initial Public Offerings, Volume in $ billions, by Quarter

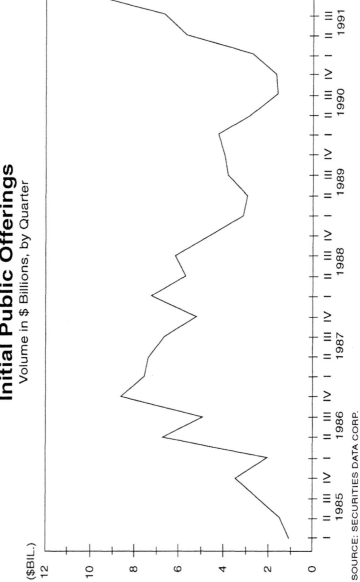

Initial Public Offerings
Volume in $ Billions, by Quarter

($BIL.)

SOURCE: SECURITIES DATA CORP.

Exhibit 6 Goldman Sachs Projected Income Statements[a]

		Year Ended December 31,	
	1991	1992	1993
Net Sales	$56,655	$59,228	$59,961
Operating expenses	52,610	54,755	55,337
Operating income	4,045	4,473	4,624
Interest income	828	890	1,058
Interest expense	52.5	38.5	24.5
Pretax income	4,821	5,324	5,657
Income taxes	1,928	2,130	2,263
Tax rate	40.00%	40.00%	40.00%
Net income	$2,893	$3,195	$3,394
Margin	5.1%	5.4%	5.7%
Earning per share	$0.87	$0.96	$1.02
Average shares outstanding	3316	3316	3316

Source: Goldman Sachs

[a]Adjusted for 2.5 to 1.0 stock split in March 1992.

Exhibit 7 Hypothetical Proceeds from an Initial Public Offering

Total for firm:		
Offer Price	14.00	16.00
Special dividend	4.52	4.52
Total per share	18.52	20.52
Shares outstanding	3,316	3,316
Total	61,421	68,054
1991 Net Income	3,749	3,749
Implied P/E Multiple	12.38	14.15
Reynolds' Proceeds:		
Shares owned	2,789	2,789
Per share proceeds:		
Stock price	14.00	16.00
Special dividend	4.52	4.52
Total per share	18.52	20.52
Total for holdings	51,645	57,222

Source: Casewriter estimates

293-084 -12-

Exhibit 8 Information about Comparable Companies

Company	Sales	Cash Flow	Operating Income[a]	Net Income	Book Value of Equity	Market Value of Equity	Total Debt	Beta
Ben & Jerry's	97.0	6.7	10.2	3.7	26.3	110.1	2.8	1.2
Dreyer's Grand Ice Cream	354.9	24.1	37.0	15.9	113.1	534.0	44.3	1.4
Empire of Carolina, Inc.	243.1	16.8	37.4	8.8	45.1	51.4	89.8	0.3
Steve's Homemade Ice Cream	35.1	2.7	3.9	1.8	11.1	37.4	3.1	2.5
Hershey Foods Corp.	2,899.2	292.3	463.0	219.5	1,335.3	4,002.5	282.9	1.0
Tootsie Roll Inds.	207.9	32.5	47.2	25.5	152.8	728.8	0.0	1.0

Source: Standard & Poor's, Compustat, and casewriter estimates.

[a]Before extraordinary items.

Eskimo Pie Corporation 293-084

Exhibit 9   Selected Financial Market Data, November 1991

I. Treasury Yields	
90 day	4.56%
Six months	4.61
One year	4.64
Five years	6.62
Ten years	7.42
Thirty years	7.92
II. Corporate Borrowing Rates	
Long-term Bond Yields	
AA	8.74%
A	9.27
BBB	9.56
BB	11.44
B	14.68
Floating Rates	
Prime rate	7.50%
Prime commercial paper (6 months)	4.76

Source: Federal Reserve Bulletin, S&P Bond Guide.

Index

S

U